So whats the Story...!

So what's the Story...?

A RESOURCE BOOK FOR
CHRISTIAN REFLECTION
AND PRACTICE

BARBARA GLASSON
AND CLIVE MARSH

The **Methodist** Church

DARTON·LONGMAN + TODD

First published in 2019 by
Darton, Longman and Todd Ltd
1 Spencer Court
140 – 142 Wandsworth High Street
London SW18 4JJ

Publication is by arrangement with
The Methodist Church
Methodist Church House
25 Marylebone Road
London NW1 5JR

ISBN: 978-0-232-53406-1

A catalogue record for this book is available from the British Library

Designed and produced by Judy Linard
Printed and bound in Great Britain by Bell & Bain, Glasgow

CONTENTS

ACKNOWLEDGEMENTS

This was an exciting project to put together following our election as President and Vice-President of the British Methodist Conference for 2019-20. As we have both published books in the past, we felt that this was a moment to use our experience to create a resource to challenge, stimulate and inspire the Church.

We are very grateful to so many people who have supported and encouraged us, in particular: David Moloney and Helen Porter at DLT; Martin Ashford, Trey Hall and Viv Wickham at Methodist Church House; and Jane Craske and Rachel Starr at the Queen's Foundation, Birmingham, who devoted considerable time at very short notice to read our efforts with a critical eye and help us to refine our text.

We want to express special thanks to David Glasson for the cover (which he both span and photographed!); and to Jill Marsh for careful reading and critique of Clive's chapters; and to both David and Jill for their continuing patience and support.

We are thankful to all those faithful people who have walked with us over many years, given their testimony to us, and lived in ways that have inspired our own life stories.

Clive and Barbara
4 February 2019

INTRODUCTION

This is a book about stories and a book of stories. It is a collection of thoughts, insights, wisdom and struggles that we have both witnessed and lived. It is a reflective book and also a resource book. We hope it will not only set you thinking, but also get you telling your own stories. We trust that it will bring to light your faith story and hold it once again alongside the stories of God. Most of all we intend this book to inspire you!

As two Methodist theologians, our life stories are very different. Clive began as a would-be linguist, but switched from German to theology when he discovered how influential German theology had been on Western thought. He's an urban person, grew up in what, at the time was labelled an 'Urban Priority Area', and has spent most of his life in education of some kind, usually trying to get people who say 'that's not for me' interested in theology. Trained in Agricultural Sciences, God has lobbed Barbara into many unusual situations for most of her ministry – from a Bread Church in Liverpool to Touchstone, an Interfaith Centre in the middle of Bradford, from work with survivors of abuse, to ministerial training in Pakistan. Her PhD is in pastoral theology and her ministry has been amongst many people the church might consider 'on the edge'. Although we have been trained differently and express ourselves differently, at the heart of it all, we are both followers of Jesus, the great story teller. Our faith has mingled with our varied experiences – the joyful and the struggling parts, the moments of elation and despair. Central to of all this has been the conviction that God's story is profoundly a narrative of love and grace.

The book is not an amalgam of our two voices. We both speak separately and differently. For information, whilst we both contributed to Chapter 2, Barbara wrote Chapters 5, 7-9 and 12, and Clive wrote 1, 3-4, 6 and 10-11. You may find that some chapters are easier for you than others, depending on your own approach to learning. As such, it's roller coaster of a book, so if something is too tricky, just skip it and keep going! We are hoping to provoke conversations around your family dinner table, in your church group, or with your friends. This is why we have punctuated each chapter with 'Points of Connection' and 'Points of Reflection'. They are opportunities to pause in the text and listen to how your soul is being stirred.

If you are using the book in a small group, make sure that the conversations are held in a safe, confidential and open way. Be aware that some of the topics are difficult – like Barbara's section on abuse – and be mindful that people often have parts of their personal stories that are painful to hold, or which they may choose not to share. Try to have an open spirit, where people are free to express doubts, struggles as well as give good testimony to God's place in their lives. Try to speak out of your own experience and not interpret other people's experience to your own ends.

You will find that some of the stories we have shared will be cracked open to look at the meanings around and within them. Others are just stories that are written without explanation. Like all stories, they come out of particular contexts but speak more widely, they are both 'told' and 'heard'.

More than anything else, we hope this book energises

and inspires you. We would love our Presidential year to be a springboard for the Church to tell stories of faith far and wide, and to explore them, and what lies beyond them, in multiple ways. And we hope that you find this book a useful resource in your personal and collective faith journeys.

Barbara and Clive
31 January 2019

Chapter 1

TELLING STORIES: WHY DO IT?

This chapter, written by Clive, sets up the whole adventure we are inviting you on in this book, by asking why we tell stories at all. What are we up to exactly? What different kinds of stories do we tell and why? This sets the scene for our exploration of how Christian thought and practice interweave with the stories we tell.

We tell stories for a variety of reasons. If we want a record of an event, we describe what happened. In this sense we want to offer a witness statement, as best as we can, of what actually happened. This is story as historical account. We narrate in the hope of capturing the truth of what occurred. There are other ways in which we can try and gain a full picture of what actually happened in a particular time or place – photographs, for example; but verbatim accounts of what people believe they saw, or what they think happened, remain crucial. Even if it may be difficult to establish the facts of a historical event, and perspectives come into play, and interpretations intervene, stories still have to be told.

We also tell stories to make sense of things, be it our own lives, other people's lives, places, ideas. We try and capture the spirit of someone if we tell a story about them. The story may not be a wholly accurate historical account of something that a person did. It may be something that they may well have done, because it sounds like the kind of thing they could have done. It captures their character. When we tell a story of our own lives, we try and express something of its meaning and purpose by picking out the key events that have shaped who we are. We say more about ourselves in the next chapter by doing precisely this. Here, right at the start, though, we note simply that we are *selective* about what we include from our personal histories when we tell our own stories. The story we offer is a composite picture of key elements that we choose to put into a narrative. 'This,' we are saying, 'is who I am.' People present themselves on the basis of what they consider to be the most significant aspects of their life-history. Telling meaning-making stories, then, requires us to make significant decisions about what to say and what not to say.

We tell stories to persuade. We want to influence others and pass on narratives that we believe will help others in their decisions about how to behave. Aesop came up with (or passed on) lots of fables not only to keep people entertained. This was moral education. It is no accident that religious narratives (and myths and parables) are often assumed primarily to be this kind of story only. Religion and morality are then seen sometimes to be virtually identical. Religions do shape people's behaviour. But religious stories, or stories told by religious people, are not simply moral tales. At their best, religions pass on stories which make clear that human beings are not always good, and then add to the stories rituals within which ways of handling human foibles and fallibilities become possible. Whilst religions do try to help people behave better, that is not the straightforward purpose of all the stories they pass on.

We tell stories, too, to entertain. We tell jokes – sometimes long, convoluted funny stories, with punch-lines (often corny) and neat twists. We tell stories for pleasure: to shock, to pass the time, to enjoy the sounds we create by telling, or to see the enjoyment of those who listen. We tell stories to make people laugh, or just to lighten the mood. There can, then, be an element of story-telling which entails the sheer pleasure of the telling and the listening. Sometimes this kind of story-telling can be risky. We may want to hear the laughter and, in the process, put on hold our ethical sensitivities. That's why jokes and stories that are sexist and racist can get passed on 'without thinking'. How do we know what is appropriate to pass on, and to whom? Laughter fudges boundaries. It can also confirm or create them.

We tell stories to build and sustain communities. Whether the communities around which stories form relate to family and kinship ties, or groups we have chosen to belong to (friends, neighbours, teams, faith groups, political parties or campaigning groups, for example), these narratives are all crucial to supporting the identities we claim for ourselves. It's important, when families get together, to tell familiar stories both of family-members still alive and of loved ones who may be long dead. These are reminders of a family's history. They help preserve a memory of what a family has experienced. There may be both joy and pain in a family's story, and some of the factual details may be a bit murky. But the stories shape family members' values and identities. What is the notion of communion of saints if not an inter-generational community of friends stretching over thousands of years?

It is no different with groups to which we choose to belong – churches included. Stories that are community-shaping are partly historical (they seek to remind us what happened), partly help us make sense of things (they attach meaning to particular events as the story of a group gets passed on) and they also contribute to our identities. We are to a great degree the sum total of the groups we belong to, and especially if there are groups to which we devote a lot of time and effort.

The community-shaping aspect of stories can, though, be double-edged. For what if the groups we belong to are not necessarily life-enhancing? What if our family stories contain such pain and trouble that the memories of family experience are not positive ones? Even if they do contain painful memories, they still need telling. One of the challenges of such story-telling will be learning how to live with, and to respond to, such stories. A recent UK example is Leicester City Football club, whose story now contains a Premier League win and the tragic death of its owner, along with four colleagues, in a helicopter crash.

We shall say more about all of these reasons for story-telling in later chapters. For the moment let's note the variety of forms of stories, and think in a very general way about how stories and story-telling relate to what we do within the Christian faith.

POINT OF REFLECTION
What sort of stories do you find yourself telling most? Do you even know? Pay attention, in the next few days, to what you say in conversation. What sort of stories are you telling?

Story-telling and/as Christian practice
It is easy to see how all of the forms of story and story-telling just identified have Christian forms. Religions have histories and stories of people from the past are crucial in the traditions that people pass on. Christianity inherits stories from Jewish

tradition about important figures (patriarchs, kings and prophets, for example). Whatever the historical accuracy of Old Testament accounts about Abraham, Sara, Hagar, Joseph, Moses, Deborah, David, Solomon, Ruth, Naomi, Elijah, Isaiah and Jeremiah, they are stories that attempt to make sense of experience even whilst the narratives about them are serving other purposes too. They are not wholly *unhistorical* stories, even whilst they are not *simply* historical accounts of these figures. They come from and serve real communities.

The same can be said of the Gospels. Accepting that Jesus existed, and that the early Christians did try to pass on reliable information about him does not turn the Gospels into modern historical records. They contain historical material, but are not simply history in the modern sense of the term. We will say more on this in Chapter 6.

Telling our own stories is vital as we make sense of our own life-experience. As we shall see in Chapter 4, simply narrating our life's key events doesn't necessarily turn our own story into a testimony. We are, though, going to want to locate our own stories within the Christian tradition in some way. We want to claim the Christian story for ourselves, for it will help us make sense of who we are and what life is about. Slotting our own personal stories (life histories) into the Christian tradition could mean forcing them inappropriately into a particular format. ('I, too, am a pilgrim who endures many things as I progress through life ...'.) At its best, locating our stories within a religious tradition is about how we learn to interpret our lives in the light of others. In this way, we gain a better sense of what God is doing in and for us as we go through life. Care will be needed so that we do not misconstrue our experience or twist it so that it cannot be helpfully shaped.

Telling stories to persuade sounds a bit dominating. But it need not be. Politicians are expected to fashion their words in such a rhetorical way as to influence others. Rhetorical flourishes designed to persuade are therefore not problematic in themselves. At issue is whether what is being commended is worth commending. Similarly, religious people are bound to think that their beliefs are worth passing on, and that others should believe like them. The stories they tell may too easily be assumed to be true and right because of the authority some hearers will attach to them. Let's face it: it is why religions can be so dangerous. The persuasiveness of political and religious rhetoric is therefore both compelling and problematic at one and the same time. We need to be wary! Stories which seek to persuade thus need to be argued about publicly. They have to defend themselves in a public arena. This is not necessarily with the intent to show that they are the only true or truthful account of what humanity is, or what reality is like. In their quest for truth and truthfulness, however, they invite people to respond: 'Yes, that's it! That's exactly how life is!' So even if the dangerous tendency of religious stories has to be acknowledged, it is also important to recognise their persuasive intent and persuasive power. They are clamouring for acceptance.

What about funny stories? Religion and humour don't often go together. More precisely, it's easier to be funny *about* religion than it is to be funny *within* religion. We would, though, be wrong to overlook the fact that stories do entertain, and that this should affect our enquiries. In examining Christian stories and the Christian Story we need to ask ourselves how this element is part of how tradition is passed on. Dullness is not necessarily a virtue! The Hebrew Bible itself has humorous material (Balaam's talking ass springs to mind). When its material is contained within the Christian Bible as the Old Testament, therefore the humour count of biblical material goes up considerably. The New Testament is not exactly a joke book, even if some of Jesus' material was clearly intended to raise a smile (camels and needles, for example) – and Jesus was Jewish after all.

The community-building aspect of stories is very, very familiar to churches. Churches are communities of people, even if they may differ from each other markedly in the level of intimacy with which members know each other. The differences may be due to scale: small communities' stories, be they rural or urban, are often more intense than those of the more anonymous larger congregations in cities. Culture, class, geography and ethnicity can also come into play: suburban congregations may tell their stories differently from churches in working-class communities; are people local, and walk to church, or do they drive in to worship; Black and Asian Christians may tell their stories quite differently from each other. Even if it is mistaken to generalize in sweeping ways, the different ways in which stories are told to maintain and uphold communities have to be recognised and respected. There is no one right way to tell a Christian story at local level. There can be unhelpful and misleading ways, but to tell a community-building, and community-maintaining story, about a Christian community need not be about a simple narration of facts. There is a story-line to a congregation. Such a story could include stories of past members, with part-historical, part-fictional elements, spun in such a way as to tell something about key figures, giving a flavour of what they were like. The purpose may be to communicate a sense of how the person came across and to communicate something of the mood of the community in which they have been significant. The hope is that such story-telling might make the contemporary community compelling and attractive to join. Local stories are part of the overarching story of the Church, itself a story of an international, cross-generational movement which has marched, and sometimes limped, through time.

These key types of story – relating to history, biography, personal experience, powers of persuasion, humour, community – are all features of the way that stories work in Christianity. So far, though, this all sounds good and positive. What about when people lie, and try and deceive with stories? Won't that need to part of the picture too?

Telling Tales

It is striking that for all the positive functions of stories and story-telling, the phrase 'telling tales' in English indicates a fundamentally negative aspect of story-telling. Tale-tellers sounds relatively neutral as a term for those who tell stories. But 'telling tales' has come to mean spouting untruths, particularly about other people. This being so, it turns stories which have a persuasive intent into manipulative acts. 'Fake news' is a very contemporary version of this. Whilst the term itself has become ambiguous – Does it mean a lie or sheer fabrication? Or a story which may not be untrue but is misleading and distracting? – it has become a term which makes a negative value-judgment of someone else's story-telling. The claim is being made that 'your story is not worth hearing' or 'your version of things is misguided'.

The tricky aspect of all of this is that telling tales in the more neutral sense of the term is totally acceptable. Spinning yarns is okay. It is a pleasurable thing to do both because of the art entailed in doing it, and in seeing the enjoyment of listeners. Throughout this first chapter we have drawn attention at a number of points to the ways that religious stories are not just about history. Because they have other purposes too, fact and fiction interweave all the time, and that's okay. The fictional elements, at their best, are not there as part of narratives in order to deceive or distort but to accentuate what is known (or believed) historically, or claimed to be true metaphysically (that is, beyond what we know factually, and therefore including what is believed about God). We can't talk about God in exactly the same way as we might talk about whether or not a bus did or did not run at a particular time and place, and so the telling of tales about God is inevitably a part of faith. The tales referred to here are stories about people who believe in God, or fictional stories which try and capture something of God in indirect ways.

It may, then, be hard to distinguish, at times, between truthful tales – historical or not – told about God, and fake news or the telling of tales to deceive. One of the things we shall therefore need to bear in mind throughout our exploring of what the Story is that we want to tell, is how we test for truthfulness.

POINT OF REFLECTION

How do we know which stories are to be passed on? What happens to stories that we create (as preachers), or pass on (as Christians who build up narratives)? When does 'tale-telling' become gossip of the wrong kind (Proverbs 11:13; 20:19?

POINT OF CONNECTION

Think of a story told to you within the life of the church that you have never been sure whether to believe. It may or may not have happened as told. Ask yourself whether or not it matters. Does it work as a story, either characterizing accurately the people being spoken about, or passing on something important about the congregation being described? What do you make of that now?

Stories and Myths

It would be wrong to finish this opening chapter without reminding ourselves of the term 'myth'. Scholars often talk of religious narratives as 'myths'. 'Myth' is a tough word because when people say something is 'just a myth', they mean it didn't happen. The difficulty is that some of the greatest works of literature ever written 'didn't happen'. Historical novels like *War and Peace* are spun around historical events. But as a story it is fictional. So we shouldn't be afraid of the word 'myth' in faith. Myths are necessary. In some ways our task needs to be aspiring to create myths! It would be great to think that between us we could come up with great stories which may or may not be about things which happened, but which pass on truths about God. 'Truth' is not simply an issue about whether or not things did or did not take place. Truth is to do with being able to speak about love, justice, peace, righteousness, joy, compassion, meaning, purpose in all sorts of different ways. Sometimes the exploration of such vital concepts occurs in story form. That is why myths are part of religion.

Our job in this book is to help each other tell truthful stories, and to do so in a way that relates them to God. The 'God stories' we connect with enable the stories we tell to come fully to life, as both stories and lives. In doing this we shall also, incidentally, be getting inside how theology works.

PRAYER

Word of God, Word of Life
Give us words with which to celebrate
To explore
To describe
To entertain
To witness
To question
To shape
To influence
To be truthful at all times.
In the name of Jesus Christ, the truth-teller, we pray.

Chapter 2

SHAPING STORIES: NARRATING LIFE EXPERIENCES

We can't really talk about stories, or encourage people to be open about their life stories, and then also ask people to think about how their life stories might be or become testimonies, and how they fit in with 'the' Christian story, without telling you something of our own. So in this chapter, we introduce ourselves.

Barbara writes...

When my parents got engaged my father was dying. Born at the outbreak of the First World War, he had contracted TB in early adult life and there was no cure. He was, however, busily studying for his Chartered Accountancy and Hospital administration exams so he wasn't exactly languishing in the sanatorium. My mother was the local librarian.

Their engagement therefore was both a great and foolish act. A romantic tragedy around which my mother shaped much of the rest of her life. The fact that Streptomycin was soon to be discovered, that my father had a lung removed and was filled full of said antibiotics, had a determined spirit and subsequently lived well into his eighties never really changed the narrative. The theme music of my upbringing was set.

Ancestors, silences and migrations

Of course, I am personally very glad my Dad survived, not least because he gave me so much more than life itself. He gave me a resilient spirit that learned to take one day at a time, because that is all you might be given. And he gave me a quizzical take on life which has stood me in good stead as my personal life narrative has taken many twists and turns of its own. I was deeply loved by both my parents and am eternally grateful for their wisdom and cherishing. And they also brought me to the realisation that if you really want to know what makes someone tick, you need to meet the ancestors!

My mother's romantic tragedy had a particular sort of nobleness about it. And I think she, in turn had acquired this from her Methodist family. There was virtue in stoicism. This was not only the result of having lived through the Second World War, it was a Methodist thing. A random memory of my own childhood is being a Brownie and learning how to make tea for 80 people in a tea urn. On reflection, I see this was something that was instilled upon us by the make do and mend environment that we inherited. We needed always to be prepared for emergencies, and the response to most emergencies seemed to be tea! I am relieved to say that I have, up to now, never been called upon to make tea in such quantity (with tealeaves) for unexpected random multitudes! Stoicism was a virtue, being able to make ends meet, not giving up, finding a way through. But my generation was also born into a great silence. We knew there had been a war, but it was something nobody was discussing. War had dislocated our parents' narrative. There were lots of things that weren't to be mentioned, there were taboos, there was an unspoken grief, there was guilt. All of this was just normal, because as a child everything is just normal, even abnormality. To be Methodist, for us, was, about this sort of nobleness. We were given lots of examples of this in Sunday School in the shape of noble people doing noble things and usually dying nobly in the process. The narrative was of sacrifice for a greater cause, preferably one for which it was possible to die, or at least lose your sight.

There also lurked an unspoken threat of shame, which it turned out was the penalty for not being noble. And this was gender specific. In particular, girls had the responsibility for sexual nobleness and literally bore the consequences for any transgressions. This was one of the great silences around, or whispered over tea and biscuits, others included madness, running off with a member of the choir, homosexuality, schizophrenia, miscarriage or postnatal depression.

Linked in with the stories of the ancestors, were stories of migrations. My aunt, who had taken herself off to Manchester University to acquire a French degree, when women just didn't do that sort of thing, had ended up teaching in Bermuda. Uncle Brian, who early in his childhood had famously announced that he had unearthed a Roman's false teeth in the garden, had taken up a career in archaeology, Auntie Thelma had caught a ship to South Africa to marry the harbour master in Durban. Stories of journeys and migrations drew the lines to the world 'out there'. These narratives were also linked to class, status and sometimes to shame. These things gave the storyline by which our family tree had its branches extended to encompass the rest of the world

Ancestors, silences and migrations have always been the starting point for stories. The ancestors might be mythological figures, biblical patriarchs, characters in books, as well as the historic anomalies in our own family history. Silences can be the source of speculation and intrigue, taboos, oversights as well as missing people. Migrations can be epic journeys or personal transformations. And all this can be linked to values such as nobleness or shame, courage, cowardice or sacrifice. They form the warp of the fabric into which threads of our life-narratives are woven.

Place

Stories are also linked to place. I think this happens in a number of ways. Firstly, places remind us of events, so returning to scenes of childhood will bring long-forgotten memories back to mind. The light, sound and smells associated with particular environments will recall and connect events in fresh ways. Our physical environment prompts our story as our personal experiences spiral around their source to be revisited and reinterpreted. Some stories even belong to a place, they can be told nowhere else; the place is sacred in that it contains a truth that cannot be divulged anywhere else. This is why it is sometimes important for people struggling to discover their own stories to return physically to where they were first enacted.

Place is also important in relation to geography. I grew up in Kent, a county with sea on three sides. I always had an awareness that I lived near the edge, that I was never far from a coastline, that there was always a big space not far away. I also had a wide view to hand, I could see beyond the immediate, I was not confined. This sense of being an edge-dweller has been with me all my life. I am seriously claustrophobic; in a confined building I am happiest in the attic. I need to have wide vistas of ideas. I love the coast, the smell and promise of the sea, the eternal nature of the ocean. To be able to see the sea is always having the knowledge that I can still set sail. It pulls.

Another way that place is important to the way we construct stories, is that it gives us routes.

Because I get my bearings from the edge, when I was in Liverpool I would always get my sense of direction by driving everywhere via the Dock Road. But local Scousers would have different routes. They would tell me to 'turn left where the cinema used to be' or always go via Auntie Madge's old house. The way we travel from A to B is intimately linked with the stories we hold, of past relationships and memories. The Australian Aboriginal people call these story routes 'songlines' and their stories are intimately related to migrations and stories associated with sacred sites.

So, the songlines of my life have had various melodies, influenced by ancestors, silences, migrations and place. At one level I am a typical product of the aspiring middle classes, at another I have made choices to leave my roots and become more freelance in following the gospel. My life story has been reconfigured by the theology I have read, by the people of faith I have met and by the 'twists and turns of outrageous fortune'. And, there's still more to sing!

Clive writes ...

Uncle Tom was not my immediate uncle, but as in most working-class families, all sorts of people were uncles and aunts, some being relatives of some kind, others being close family friends. Uncle Tom was a Methodist, though I didn't know it at the time. At some point in my childhood, eavesdropping on a conversation he was engaged in at our house, about someone who'd not behaved very well, and had 'gone down the wrong path', I have a memory of Uncle Tom reminding us all 'but he's another person for whom Christ died'. I wasn't too well up at that stage on atonement theories, and the different ways of understanding the possible meanings of the death of Jesus. Yet somehow, in and from that conversation, I managed to grasp that Uncle Tom meant 'everyone'... literally everyone, in the sense that anyone and everyone could have access to the saving work of God in and through Jesus Christ. It was, I now realize, a truth about humankind which people 'get at' from different angles and with different purposes. Lots of people access the insight about human equality through the reminder that all are 'made in the image of God'. Being reminded that Christ died for all is a way of getting at the same truth 'from the other end', if you like: we're all sinful, and need rescuing in some way, from whatever it is that drags us down.

The juxtaposition of warmth and harshness in working-class life can sometimes be a shock to people who haven't lived it, though the glimpse of the reach of God's grace present in my Uncle Tom story occurred in the context of a very ordinary working-class upbringing in North-West England. I am much more assertive and explicit now than I often have been in the past about my roots. That's because there are aspects of it which I have only begun to process explicitly for myself in recent years. It's also to do with having more confidence about owning up to who I am, how I've been shaped, what's been a struggle, and the fact that I don't need to pretend any more that I'm something I might not be. There is no doubt I have sometimes had to 'play a role' in the multiple middle-class worlds I've lived in: education, work, the church. I often say, when referring to academic conferences I go to, that the two words that fill me with dread are 'Drinks Reception'. I have been propelled into a world of chit-chat and sherry-sipping in which I still feel uncomfortable. My upbringing and my student years did not prepare me for this, and it never really occurred to me that such occasions might be part of church culture too. Give me a mug of tea and an informal setting any day! I have had to get used to it. I also have to accept that I am myself middle-class now in so far as social mobility, education, income took me into new social and professional worlds. I am not always uncomfortable! People who share a similar journey to mine, though, often report on the split identities they have to carry with them.

All of this has taught me that the social culture of those

who run events (in organisations of all kinds, including churches) may well dictate how an organization comes over. If, then, the church exists primarily for its non-members, as has often been rightly claimed, how are we going to get beyond the culture and cultures of those who are in it already, and especially those who 'pull its strings'? Or who is going to help shape the culture of the church's events if we're meant to be 'for others'? This is what has led me to keep on looking closely at how theology and popular culture inter-relate. Whose culture matters, or is seen to matter? How is theology being influenced by cultures of all kinds? And if God can be present in and through all cultures ... then what?

Whiteness and Identity

My class background has left me with a chip on my shoulder. But it's been invaluable in helping me wrestle with the multiple factors that make up our identity as human beings. It took me some time to start to process the privilege which took effect early to help me get to university. I'd been nudged and supported in various ways since the age of 7 or 8 ('he's good at sums!') to do well in exams, ended on 'the right side of the fence' in the great 11+ divide in the early 1970s, was steered in a particular direction simply because of being considered to be 'bright' in a certain way. I was aware that other pupils lived in posher parts of town, but they weren't necessarily bright. I was also aware that some came from really tough areas, and had complex family backgrounds, but were sometimes really bright and smart. I wonder how contemporary initiatives in 'Widening Participation' (getting people from neighbourhoods from which people don't usually go to university) would have played out in the classes I belonged to between the ages of 7 and 18

What was largely absent in my upbringing was ethnic diversity ... save, that is, for our next door neighbour from

Dar es Salaam. I have as a result sometimes made quite naïve judgments about my Whiteness. I was lacking in experience of how to relate to people with a different ethnic background from mine. And let's face it: like many other (all?) parts of Britain in the 1960s and 1970s, working-class Merseyside was racist, sexist and homophobic. I didn't know the word 'homophobic' till much later. Nor was I conscious of knowing anyone homosexual; they'd have needed great guts to come out. I did know that to suggest anyone was gay would have been seen as an insult.

The layers of privilege, though, were already in place for me: maleness, Whiteness, aspiring (as opposed to impoverished) working-class, educational opportunities. Tangled up with leaving home, and with expanding educational horizons, came stark challenges to my own racism. I spent three months in Chicago when I was a student, studying at a theological college on the south side of the City in what is, in effect, an extended educational campus between 51st Street in the North and 59th Street in the South, and bounded on the East by Lake Michigan, and on the West by Washington Park. The message given to all students (all white students only? I'm not sure I ever knew) was simple: 'Here's a security whistle. If you are accosted, especially after dark, go to the centre of the street, and blow the whistle repeatedly. Do not, under any circumstances go south of 59th Street, and do not under any circumstances alight from public transport North of 51st Street until you reach Downtown.' The implication was (I wonder what was actually said at the time?): these areas are poor and black. You will be relatively safe in the (largely white) educational haven between 51st and 59th Street, but take no chances.

Of course, I was reluctant to be bound by this. It took me many weeks to pluck up courage, and needed many conversations with other students, black and white, to assure me it would be okay, but I *did* want to walk South of 59th Street. We had been given advice on practical security grounds, though it never occurred to me at the time that even feeling I had the freedom to roam where I wanted could itself be seen as a statement of white privilege. However, using my freedom to roam taught me a major lesson about the insidious, fear-driven, irrational basis of my own racism.

One Saturday, I walked South of 59th Street. I was suddenly the only white face. I don't recall any major interest in my presence, but I was nervous. A well-dressed (suited) black man came towards me on the same side of the street. Just as I was about pass him, he put his hand inside his jacket. 'This is it', I thought, as I anticipated the size of the weapon he would be drawing out. Instead, he pulled out a sheet of paper and asked very matter-of-factly whether I could point him to a particular address he was looking for.

Relative poverty

A second Chicago story links my growing awareness of the interplay of ethnicity, class, material well-being, the hiddenness of forms of deprivation, and the sheer power of assumptions we may hold about others. I took part in a class that enabled me to gain an insight into issues in US society and theology. It was my first experiential introduction to forms of liberation theology (Latin American, Black, Feminist). When I was introduced to the group, and opened my mouth, a conversation ensued about my 'cute' accent. The students (of varying ages) also pointed out to me what the benefits were of my having such an accent in American society: I'd be trusted, assumed to be intelligent, 'known' to have good connections. It also became apparent that assumptions were being made about my social background: I was from the University of Oxford, I was white, I was English ... so I must be middle- to upper-class and wealthy. Hidden aspects were rather different, of course. I wanted to explain (and trumpet!) the importance to me of Merseyside, of my working-class background. I also wanted to highlight the fact that I'd been able to get to Chicago only by the skin of my teeth, financially, through an anonymous donation from someone in the church (filtered through a supportive chaplain – another privilege, I admit). At that time I lacked the confidence to spell all this out. They remained hidden aspects of my Chicago experience, though they shaped me and my faith profoundly. I saw the interplay of poverty, class and ethnicity more keenly than ever in Chicago and actually felt some of it – even whilst being privileged. I was skint for a time when it looked as though I was nothing of the sort. It also helped me review my upbringing and think about how I'd approach life in the future.

I've never been stony broke since. But my family's finances were often fragile both before and after I left home. I've also been a member of churches for most of my life which have kept me alongside people with little money and few means. It's been an important part of my Christian journey. I have been enabled to realize that while material matters don't save us, the lack of them may prevent people from hearing the voice of God at all.

Living in Leicester

Preparing to move to Leicester in 2004 I was shocked to hear people saying to me, 'Don't you need a passport to go there?', a further reminder of the way that racism takes shape. Leicester was being assumed to be a foreign county within 'our' midst. It didn't, however, take us very long to decide to move when my wife was offered a church position there. It was a chance for us all, as a family, to be enriched by religious and ethnic diversity and to move into a city again. Leicester has brought us neighbours and friends of many faiths and none and, in my case, the chance to teach groups of adults comprising the currently religious (of different faiths), the ex-religious, the anti-religious, and those plainly bewildered by religion. Those teaching sessions have enriched us all. I think the story of the Kingdom of God – which stretches our current experience into God's future – has to be multi-faith. This doesn't mean I believe all religions are saying the same thing, that religions are all equal, or that religion is always a good thing. But the wonderful rich complexity of religious diversity surely means that Christians still have things to learn, from God through others. 'The' Christian story itself continues to get more and more diverse as time goes on.

POINT OF REFLECTION

If you think of your own life story what are the theme tunes and songlines you have sung? What opinions and prejudices have you had to revisit? What really makes you thankful?

PRAYER
Thanks be to God
For the story told in me
For the story held in me
For the story entrusted to me.
Help me to tell it
To honour it
To celebrate it
To live it
For the love of Jesus.

Chapter 3

CONNECTING STORIES: MAKING CHRISTIANITY OUR OWN

In this chapter, Clive looks at how the Bible and the Christian tradition are used in practice as we seek to interpret our life experience. We locate our own stories within the understandings of God and the stories which Christianity carries with it. But how does that work?

The phrase 'the Christian story' slips easily off the tongue. It is understandable why people inside and outside Christianity might assume that there is a basic shape and content to the stories that Christians tell when using the Bible and in order to 'pass on the tradition'. A basic structure of creation-fall-redemption-consummation would be affirmed by a great many Christians as the shape of the Christian story. In other words:

- The world was brought into being
- Something went wrong
- It needed rectifying (and God enabled that to be possible)
- The world has a hopeful future (for ever) as a result.

That basic shape does not, though, tell us a great deal. It is not as helpful as it may appear in thinking how we might make practical use of it, and pass on to others, in everyday life. There are lots of other sub-plots to be told that supplement and fill in the basic story line.

There are, for example, stories to be told about how concretely God gets involved with the world which God has made ('incarnation' – enfleshment). The reason we as Christians talk about Jesus so much is that we think God was getting entangled in creation in a new and distinctive way, and that by telling Jesus-stories we shall also be telling God's story. Not only that, Jesus-stories make the God stuff accessible, *because* God became close and more available to us in Jesus. Stories about Jesus become, at one and the same time, stories about the humanity and divinity of God.

There are also stories about the creative way in which God has always been a life-giving presence, as Holy Spirit, within the material world. Such stories are likely to link with a great many different stories about human creativity in the present.

There are stories to be told about the different ways in which things have gone wrong within the created order. The whole created world is endangered. Things have gone wrong not just within individual human beings but also within the structured ways in which human beings organise themselves. There may well be a single catch-all theological term for that ('sin'), but short theological words don't easily explain themselves. Stories need telling so we have more of a chance of grasping what the doctrines are driving at.

To add to that is the fact that there are lots of different Christians traditions, often emphasizing different bits of 'the (one) Story'. Sometimes they do this explicitly: Pentecostal emphasis on the Holy Spirit, for example; sometimes by the way in which their practices imply a particular emphasis: Roman Catholic emphasis on sacraments, for instance. Such emphases shape the specific stories that are told and particular sections of the Bible, which are used to link up with those denominational stories and identities.

So we are left with multiple stories ... hundreds of them within the Bible itself, some of which are shared with Judaism, which remains a living religion alongside Christianity, some of which we inherit from early Christian tradition, and some of which have been added since – stories about Christian experience or the church tradition of saints and sinners (and that means all of us).

So how do we handle creatively the relationship and tension between the one Story and the many stories? And what are we doing when make connections with these stories, thereby locating ourselves within the 'big tent' of the one Story? That's what this chapter is about.

Point of Connection
Before we go any further, have a think about your most obvious 'points of connection' with the one (big) Christian Story. Which stories, which parts of the Bible, which aspects of Christian history have proved the most meaningful for you in your Christian life? Why is that?

The One Christian Story? Plot and sub-plots

The Bible is a rich and varied collection of all sorts of literature. We have to accept that its contents are not all stories. While we might talk, then, of the 'Christian story', the different books that make up the Bible, and the different kinds of literature it contains, can work in many and diverse ways to enable us to access, and become part of, the Story. Your response to the 'Point of Connection' exercise a moment ago might have been: 'Well, it's not just stories I latch onto to help me in my faith, as I try and understand my life. I use letters; I use the Psalms; I latch on to sayings of Jesus. It's not just stories that help me.' That's right. That *is* how it works. For the purposes of this book, however, we need to speak of the Christian Story as a whole, and we need to see the Bible as a key resource for getting inside that Story, even if the Bible, and the Christian traditions that flow from and build on it are very varied indeed. To talk of one Big Story and lots of sub-plots allows, then, for the fact that all sorts of spoken, written, visual, and musical materials carry the Story, even if the Bible, in all its own complexity and diversity, has a special place. How, though, do we in practice get inside the one Story? In answering that question we shall be providing a bridge to the next chapter, which explores how we tell our own Christian story.

Even recognising that the Bible is rich, complex and diverse, it can also be said to contain a single plot. That plot relates to the basic Story identified in the previous section. But do you agree? How would *you* characterise the Bible's single plot: 'God saves the world'? 'God loves the world?' Even if you say, 'Well, those two statements are basically saying the same thing', they are already differing ways of shaping an interpretation of the sixty-six books that make up the Protestant Canon. As soon as you utter whichever four-word formulation of the Bible's central plot you prefer, the questions begin.

Here are some of those questions. Will God actually succeed in saving the world, or might humanity be able to mess things up so badly that we stop what God wants for the world? If God will save the world, will that happen regardless of what we do? And, if so, what's the point of believing, then? If God is to save the world, is God somehow dependent on us – to some extent at least – because 'God has no hands but our hands'? Does that mean we somehow *do* contribute to our own salvation? Yet doesn't that sound a bit dodgy – as if we're getting a bit too above ourselves? If God does indeed save, *how* does that come about?

We may not want to address any of these questions. In practice, we get on with daily life and our thoughts, decisions, emotions and actions are influenced and shaped by the faith we carry with us. We may not think through how this happens, but the Bible and the Christian tradition will not let us off the hook. *By its very form*, as a rich collection of materials for us to engage with, it poses questions. In order to tell 'the one Christian story', Christians have to tell other stories (sub-plots) too. All of the sub-plots of the one Story become important features of Christianity's main 'point' (that God loves/saves the world) without which the 'story of salvation' would be difficult to understand. Stories that fill out and make the one basic story of salvation come alive are essential to enable hearers (us!) to grasp a bit more about how salvation works. There may be different understandings of what people need saving *from* and saving *for*. One thing is for sure: we need lots of stories to enable the story of God's loving and saving of the world to be made to live in us and to be passed on. We shall also want other people alongside us, putting their interpretations next to ours, on the journey.

POINT OF REFLECTION

Have a think about how, and how regularly, you read the Bible. What habits of Bible-reading do you have? Do you follow a structure? Do you use a lectionary? Who do you look at the Bible with? What kinds of groups are there that you are part of, or could join, to stimulate your exploration of the Bible?

I was once in an ecumenical Bible study group where, after a wide-ranging discussion of many possible ways of understanding the text before us, the group-leader clearly felt he had to draw things to a close and offer a definitive reading of the text. Without reference to any of the ideas that had been offered, he added a further interpretation. Have you had any similar experiences in Bible studies? How did you, and how do you now, respond? How do you think Bible studies best work?

Handling the sub-plots

Let us think of a few biblical examples of how some of the sub-plots of the one story of salvation actually take shape. If we start at the very beginning, the early chapters of Genesis give us a number of stories that tell us something about how we are to understand humanity's place in the created order. The stories are not, of course, a historical or scientific account of the origins of the universe or the creation of the earth. They are ways of saying: humanity is not responsible for its own existence; God is. Human life is given. But every single human who ever lived is prone to forget their dependence on God. That neglect is, we might say, the primary distortion of human self-understanding (sin), and has very severe consequences. But everyone does it. So rather than provide a scientific account of the world's origins, and whether or not these stories are offering any kind of *explanation* of how this profound forgetfulness has infected all human beings, what the stories do is set the scene. Human beings have to live with this distortion of profound and damaging forgetfulness, and will only become all that they can be as human beings by starting to remember God again. They (we!) will then be remembering in whose image they (we) are made. Telling stories about all of this, however, rather than offering abstract analyses or even uttering doctrinal statements or credal confessions, is often the best way of seizing hold of what we are trying to say. For things to 'stick' they have to be memorable, and we need to be able to connect to the content emotionally. This is an insight which will reverberate through this book!

Then there's 'the Exodus'. There's a whole biblical book bearing that name, its forty chapters containing dozens of graphic and sometimes shocking stories: an abandoned child left floating on a river, a bush that burned but didn't burn up, locusts, frogs, slavery, wilderness wanderings, law-making, tent-building … lots of compelling stuff. At the heart of the book is *the* Exodus (Exodus 14-15): the story of the people of Israel escaping captivity in Egypt. Quite what happened, when, and for how many, will never be wholly clear. It need not be disputed that something happened for a group of former slaves, in a way that proved decisive for the community and movement which became Judaism, and which has had a knock-on effect on Christianity and world history more generally. For our purposes it is less the historical facts that are significant than what was made of the event. 'The Exodus' has become a symbolic narrative for Jews, Christians and others. It is a powerful narrative which is not 'just a story' because it records what happened to a people, and echoes, when people tell it again, what continues to happen to people experiencing, and seeking to break free from, any kind of captivity. The Exodus has proved a particularly powerful narrative for African-American Christians whose ancestors were enslaved and struggled for freedom. In turn, black Christians everywhere feel able to identify with features of the story on the basis of their actual experience of daily life in the West *today*, in a way that white Christians often fail to grasp.

The Exodus reverberates through the New Testament too because of its formative role in shaping the people of Israel, understood as a living community. The Church claims a direct connection with that community and sees itself as a Messianic movement in continuation with that community, formed by Jesus Christ, whether or not Jesus actually intended to form a church of any kind. Cross and Resurrection do not replace Exodus. They echo it in a new way, whilst needing the whole history of the people of Israel as precursor to what God brought about in Christ. The entire Bible is the record of what a *people* do. The Bible becomes 'Scripture' because it functions as a book of a group: followers who gather round a story book not simply to 'listen for pleasure' but to be shaped by the book's stories, to discuss and argue with fellow listeners about the meaning, value and usefulness of these stories.

We shall look further in Chapter 6 at how Jesus' stories work, but what of Paul? Paul tells fewer stories but becomes a story by his fervent activity as a key early Christian missionary. The Book of Acts tells his story in narrative form. His letters give us the shape of his life. Paul's story is then told both as the story of Christ's continuing work in Paul's ministry and in the communities he was connected with, as the story of the emerging Church. His letters are the record of the early experiments to form communities 'in Christ': fresh attempts, in continuity with the people of Israel, to fashion human communities in the way that God wants them to be fashioned.

The stories of the New Testament are not of themselves

enough to do this. The New Testament needed the Hebrew Bible, incorporated into the Christian Bible rather misleadingly as the 'Old' Testament. Christianity cannot be properly understood without knowledge of its Jewish roots. The New Testament in turn needs supplementing. What follows won't function in the same way as biblical texts. The biblical stories are used as a kind of 'measuring rod' for stories told later. The Bible will always go on carrying more weight than other stories from the 'cross-checking' point of view. Using the Bible healthily and creatively is, however, a tricky task. It contains unwelcome and challengeable assumptions – based on patriarchy, slave-owning and ethnic cleansing. And the more immediate stories that we tell each other – of our own life-histories, of our local communities, of our families, of our church congregations, of our friendships, of political groups we belong – are always likely to be more persuasive and emotionally-engaged, to begin with at least, than any biblical stories we read and pass on. Our faith-inspired, life-shaping task is to make connections: to find out where our current stories might be informed and enriched by stories from the Bible; to probe where there is more to be discovered about the biblical stories by the experiences we have and the stories we tell each other. The interplay is crucial for a living faith and a living community.

POINT OF REFLECTION
When you think of the stories that have most influenced you in your faith, how many are biblical? What is the ratio of 'stories of other people', 'stories of famous Christians', 'stories from Christian history' to biblical stories when you reflect on the shaping of your faith?

Saints and sinners

We need, then, other stories too, beyond Jesus, Paul and the other early Christians. We need to be able to access a history of Christian saints: people who turned out to be inspirational or exemplary Christians for a whole variety of reasons, and whose stories will prompt and support us better to understand what faith is about and how we can keep hold of it, especially in tough times. The Roman Catholic, Anglican and Orthodox traditions have official lists and named saints' days. Ignatius of Antioch, Clement of Alexandria, Basil of Caesarea, Gregory of Nyssa and Augustine of Hippo may not be household names in Barnsley and Brighton now, but were prominent figures in the early Christian centuries. Their stories – and those of other saints – can be summoned up when needed as tales of early Christians whose lives and experiences proved crucial as Christianity grew and expanded.

Of course, they were men, were all bishops, and so can't exactly be said to represent ordinary life experience. But they would have been the first to remind us that they were sinners too. They didn't ask to be saints. It's just that their stories are interesting, we know something about them and they helped shape the faith we now have. Two millennia after Christianity's appearance, we have a lot of stories to work with. The stories of women saints have needed a bit of work to uncover sometimes, revealing the patriarchal world in which so much of Christian history has operated. But now, Hilda of Whitby, Hildegard of Bingen, Julian of Norwich, Teresa of Avila, Thérèse of Lisieux almost *are* household names, in Newcastle, Neath, and beyond.

Saints do not, of course, always need to be officially recognised in so far as their influence upon us is concerned. For what is a saint but a person through whom God's holiness is evident? This means that in Protestant traditions, too, influential Christians are readily called 'saints' if they prove inspirational either in their own lifetimes, or after their death. I remember many school assemblies on Albert Schweitzer, wondering where he found the time to be a medical doctor, missionary, a biblical scholar *and* an outstanding organist and interpreter of J.S. Bach's music! Martin Luther King Jr.'s life speaks deeply to black Christians everywhere but is inspirational to people – of faith and not – across all ethnic backgrounds. In the present, Malala Yousafzai is already proving inspirational to a whole range of younger people especially, and reminds us that God works through a wide variety of people.

It is vital that we get beyond the famous in thinking about who our saints are. The chances are that ordinary people's holiness has influenced us profoundly and so the life-stories of others has shaped our own stories because we have known 'saints' personally. We will, though, have known our local saints in their flawed state – as real people. This is important information to 'read back into' the lives of (the famous, 'official') saints. They were sinners too. It's reassuring. We shall be able to be realistic about our own stories and the many stories we will hear and tell. They *have* to be stories of flawed people, because that is who we are. It is only with flawed people that God works.

POINT OF CONNECTION

Who are your saints – famous or otherwise? What role have they played for you? What kind of faith have you ended up with because of their influence upon you?

One Story, many stories, our stories

Our own stories, then, slot into this vast gamut of Christian life-stories past and present, seeking to find a place within the one over-arching (flexible but capacious) Christian story. In one sense there is no limit to the number of Christian stories there can be, for there are as many Christian stories as there are Christians. A Christian is, however, someone who is trying to shape their life, and be shaped by God, as known in Christ, according to the Christian story. Simply telling a life-story, in other words, does not make one a Christian. We shall explore next what it is that turns a life-story into a testimony.

Is there, then, such a thing as 'the' Christian Story? Well: 'yes' and 'no'. Ultimately, God's Story is the only story that matters – the story that is being told, and enacted, by God as God interacts with the world (the world, note; not just human beings).

PRAYER

Living God

Make us part of your story

Connect us to the living Christ

Make the Jesus stories live in us

Breathe your spirit in and through us

So that we live the story

and your story shapes us.

Amen

Chapter 4

LIVING STORIES: STORY AS TESTIMONY

In this chapter, Clive explains what testimonies are and encourages readers to speak theirs. The chapter defines testimonies as a particular type of personal story. It shows how locating ourselves within the Christian story is a way of exploring the experience of 'new life' to which testimonies seek to bear witness.

Testimonies are accounts of people's experiences of God at work, in both bad times and good. Whether or not the stories have happy endings, just by telling the story of how God works in our lives, we bear witness to what God has done and is doing, for us personally. Mingled with all sorts of emotions – joy, sorrow, elation, struggle, despondency, contentment, relief, anger – testimonies are not delivered only by special people who have dramatic stories to tell. They are real life stories: stories of real life; stories of everyday lives in which God's presence makes a difference. It's vital *for all of us* that testimony is part of life. If some people do have dramatic stories, then so be it. Most people's Christian stories may be more ordinary; but they will still be life-shaping.

More generally in society, testimonies are known mostly

as statements that stand up in a court of law. People are asked for their versions of events, and offer sworn statements about what they think to be true. Many dictionaries start to use the word proof in defining the term. Where humans are involved, though, proof is often difficult to establish. Whilst a swollen jaw might be testimony to some considerable pain or soreness, stories functioning as testimonies do not offer the same kind of proof.

When our faith stories become testimonies, they are our life experiences interpreted and presented as examples of lives lived consciously with and for God. Testimonies are offered as accounts of lives that God has touched. They are not *explanations* of those interpretations. Nor are they fully thought-through rational accounts of exactly how and why the speaker (the witness!) believes God to have acted and be acting in a particular way. They are living expressions of our actual experiences of believing.

Sometimes, of course, an experience of God is dramatic. When people become Christian following some major turning point in life, it can be hard to tell any other story than that of their own dramatic conversion. We have all known people whose experiences are so powerful that they have personal stories to tell from which it is hard to move on: recovery from alcoholism; handling and emerging from twisted relationships; finally dealing with a debt crisis; being rescued from a disaster situation. These experiences shape people's lives so profoundly, that it is hard to imagine that there could be any other tale to tell. The feeling of 'I *was* there ... but now I am *here* ...' affects everything. If Christians who have such a life-story become preachers then they have to be careful: sermons can become nothing but testimonies. The sense of rescue (by God) is so palpable that, try as they might, the preachers cannot tell any other story but their own. It seeps into everything.

This is tricky, for why shouldn't such a dramatic story of rescue keep on affecting everything? Whether or not our own coming to faith was dramatic, shouldn't it influence our whole lives? Yes on both counts! Testimony is not, however, only about the process of coming to faith. As we shall see, we bear witness to God's activity in our lives in all sorts of ways, and at different points, not only at the start of a Christian life. So, whether dramatic or not, the stories of God's work in our lives must still be told.

POINT OF CONNECTION
What are your own first thoughts about where God has acted in your life? Was a dramatic conversion involved? Was there a clear starting point? Have there been many key events or experiences that have drawn your attention to God's activity?

What is testimony for?
What are the Christian stories that are called testimonies trying to do? What is it that is being witnessed? In what ways, if at all, are they proof of anything? In a very helpful exploration of what testimonies are, why they are important and how they work in local church life, Lillian Daniel suggests this definition: A testimony is 'a spoken story about how you… experienced God, offered in the context of … community worship'.[1] She is emphasizing two aspects: it is spoken (not written); it is offered in worship (not in some other setting). Of course, there could be other settings where testimonies can be offered: small groups, training events, concerts, music practices. But Daniel is inviting us to consider worship as the most fitting location. We shall also want to broaden the range of ways in which we can see that testimonies are

effective. They do not *only* have to be spoken. Even so, her two emphases are worth pursuing.

When testimonies are *spoken*, they live best when offered by a real person, in the presence of other real people. People may be able to write well. Videos can be made, thus producing a virtual version. But testimonies are best spoken in an actual, live setting because they are records of the experiences of people who are embodied, and live in an embodied world. If I am to ask as a hearer: 'How can this story have happened in this way? Who is this person?' it is better to hear a person in person. Even if a video is made, it is better for this to be filmed in the company of others rather than at home alone.

It is better still to hear a person in person in a context where both speaker and hearer share in the same community of worship. So *worship*, suggests Daniel, *is the best context* for the delivery and hearing of testimonies. 'Testimony', as she reminds us, 'goes so much deeper than one individual's deep thoughts.'[2] The working of God, and people's discovery of God's activity, is bound up with, and needs to be articulated in, a community of faith. Even if events have happened in daily life, it is in a faith community where experiences are explored, unpacked and interpreted.

POINT OF REFLECTION

How confident are you about speaking in public? If your answer is 'not at all' then you have a good biblical forebear. Moses said: '... I have never been eloquent, neither in the past nor even now ... I am slow of speech and slow of tongue' (Exodus 4:10). You're in good company! Our guess is, though, that you're fine in conversation with friends. There may seem a big step from informal conversation to speaking in public. 'Speaking in public' isn't, though, necessarily the same as 'public speaking' (e.g. giving a lecture, or delivering a sermon). Before the end of the chapter we'll encourage you to think about what might feature in your testimony. You'll be able to build up to thinking about how you'd prepare to tell others about your Christian experience.

For the moment, have a think about settings where you *do* enjoy talking about your experience. Why are you comfortable in that setting? Are there contexts in church life where you're happy telling others about things that happen to you, or what you're thinking about? If so, what makes them okay? If not, what makes church settings awkward?

Lillian Daniel's emphases are helpful, but we want to go further. People's accounts of their experience of God, and of God at work in their lives, can be offered in other ways: through video and audio recordings, through written accounts (letters, articles). These remain important and should not be underestimated. Whoever has a story of God should be encouraged to tell it, and with whatever form of communication they feel comfortable! Daniel's basic point has force, though, in that it reminds us that testimony is not simply about what individuals *claim* to be the case. Relating an account of God's activity to a community of faith is a way of testing it out.

Testimonies as interwoven tales

Testimony may seem a very private practice: deep convictions of the workings of God in personal life. Ultimately, though, testimonies are accounts of where people's life stories interweave with the story of creation, and of humanity, which God is unfolding in the world. People recognise in their own life experience ways in which the presence and activity of God has made a difference to how they interpret and understand themselves and their actions. By bringing their life experience alongside stories from the Bible, or alongside Christian insights and beliefs, or by making creative comparisons and associations with the life stories of other Christians, fresh 'readings' of our life stories become possible. Testimonies are an early step in that process. They are a kind of first phase of what may eventually become theological reflection.

That may, though, make the initial process of moving from experience to testimony sound a bit too rational, and too neat. It isn't meant to. Testimony often remains more immediate, more urgent. Reflection will certainly happen at some point, but the starting point of the experience of God may be feelings-based. There may be a sense of God's presence, or just a funny feeling, or a feeling of being overwhelmed, or caught up, or prompted, or encouraged, or empowered. Testimony may report on one such experience, or a series of them, and remain quite feelings-based too. It is vital then that the journey from experience to testimony to reflection does not stifle the energy of the encounter with God.

In processing such experiences, people sometimes access Christian traditions in all sorts of different ways to make the journey from experience to testimony. Some Christians know their Bibles well and so the linking of biblical characters, biblical events and biblical stories comes easily: happenings simply chime in with things that are there in the memory, because the store of knowledge of biblical materials is well-stocked. Biblical characters may then come readily to people's minds. In our experience, particular favourites people find helpful are Ruth and Naomi, Isaiah, the story of the Prodigal Son/the Forgiving Father, Mary and Martha, the Rich Young Ruler and Lydia. Others might have a developed sense of the multi-faceted Jesus story – without necessarily knowing which stories are in which Gospels. God helps people face honestly what life presents them with, and what happens to them, with reference to the Jesus story.

Other Christians latch their life stories onto the lives of famous Christians or saints. The lives, experience and insights of the Wesley brothers, or later Methodists, might prove helpful for contemporary Methodists. Testimonies might therefore include phrases like, 'as John Wesley once said in one of his sermons...', if it helps a person better understand their own experience. Yet others have a strong sense of the themes of Christian faith. The shape and content of specific doctrines, salvation, the Holy Spirit, God as Trinity may come into play as people tell their stories. A testimony-giver might say: 'The intensity and depth of the sense of community I felt made me realize what "church" as its best can be about. I felt loved, accepted, free, for the first time.' Or again: 'What it means to be "saved" only came to life when I was able to accept what I'd done, acknowledge that God had forgiven me for it, and that others accepted me too, despite what I'd done.'

In my own case, one of the biggest leaps I made in my own spiritual journey was when the questions I had posed about Christian faith became part of my faith itself. Fearing that critical questions – about the Bible, about ethical and political issues, about the church's 'out-of-touchness' would take me beyond the church – I then found myself in a setting where I met other Christians of different traditions who were asking similar questions. God enabled me to see that the church was bigger and more diverse than my limited vision, that Christ would not be offended by any question of any kind and could cope with anything, and that God's Spirit actually *wanted* me to make the exciting, critical journey. The development of a critical faith turned out not to be a criticism *of* faith, but a way of moving to a more lively faith which was able to put up with more loose ends than I originally thought possible. It was a deep, inner, emotionally-satisfying shift for me and not simply an intellectual step. I was able to live comfortably with Matthew, Mark, Luke, John, Paul, James, Mary, Martha, Lydia, Nympha, Martin, Dorothee and lots of other Christians – not all of whom agree with each other, but all of whom were followers of Jesus Christ.

In all sorts of ways, then, people interweave their personal stories with aspects of the multi-dimensional Christian story (its Bible, its traditions, its people) in order to construct their testimonies. Not all testimony will make the step very far towards reflection in this way. Nor does it have to, even if it will be tangled up in Christian tradition in some way. What, then, *are* the hallmarks of testimony? If we can get at those, then we shall have some sense of how testimonies can be shaped.

What does a testimony look like?

A testimony does not follow a single, prescribed format. Whilst a testimony has particular functions and serves specific purposes, it doesn't always have to have the same shape or content. As noted earlier, accounts of Christian experience may not necessarily be dramatic. People tell their faith stories in different ways. Beyond the fact that a testimony will witness in some way to the work of God in the life of the speaker, as perceived by that speaker, there are no rules as to what has to be included. Nor is there any order in which any particular elements have to be presented.

One important observation made by Lillian Daniel is that 'the *practice of testimony* … [turns] … out to be *testimony about practices.'*[3] By this she doesn't mean that testimonies are lists of things that people do. Speaking from a context in which testimony-giving became part of a congregation's life, she was noting that the stories of people's Christian experience inevitably interwove with their participation in church life, as well as with what may have been happening to them more broadly in life. Their congregation was their spiritual home; so, whether or not they had formal roles, their participation was important. Testimony-givers are often likely to focus on what they did in or for the church, and what became evident to them about God and their faith through that.

We can add to the observation that 'testimony (is) about practices', the insight that our Christian experience includes what we do, and what we (think we) are in control of, though will not be confined to that. If God is active in and around us, and in the wider world in which we are active, then things will happen to us which are far beyond our control, yet in and through which we believe we see God at work. This will be beyond what we choose to do in our local Christian settings. The lenses provided by the Jesus stories in the Gospels, and in the Bible as a whole, help us identify where God in Christ is at work in the world and in our lives.

Within a testimony when we say 'this happened to me, and it gave me a new life experience' we are saying we believe that God has encountered us, challenged us, supported us, lifted us up.

POINT OF REFLECTION
In what does a testimony consist? Methodist evangelist Trey Hall has come up with some helpful 'dos and don'ts' which we are adapting here.

What would my own testimony look like? (10 rules of thumb):

- Aim for 4-5 minutes.
- Prepare in advance; take time to reflect and map it out; practise it aloud, so you can feel comfortable with it, and make it part of you, before you offer it publicly.
- Remember it's *your* testimony (no one else's).
- Don't worry whether it's funny or profound. It's *your* story. Tell it like it is!
- It will include a 'new life' experience of some kind (at whatever life-stage your change of heart, new insight or dramatic conversion happened), remembering that 'new life' may not mean 'happy ending'. God may have helped you to 'live with' some tough stuff which isn't resolved, and that's the testimony you want to give.
- If your story does contain painful memories within it, 'speak from your scars not from your wounds'. In other words, do some processing first. Think deeply around what's been happening to you with the help of others. It may take a bit of time to get ready to offer your testimony.
- Be honest.
- Don't be disrespectful of, or hostile towards, other Christian traditions or other religions.
- Be yourself.
- Try and enjoy the experience of the telling!

In trying to enjoy the experience of telling your story, however nervous you might be, the likelihood is that your story will unlock the courage of others to tell theirs. God will be able to use even your nervousness.

'Use words if you have to'

Is testimony evangelism? There's the famous saying, ascribed to Francis of Assisi (amongst others): 'Go into all the world and preach the Gospel. Use words if you have to.' In other words, faith-sharing is not necessarily a spoken thing. We share faith by actions, habits, dispositions, gestures too. So if testimonies are spoken, this suggests that testimonies and evangelism are to be distinguished. Is this so? They certainly overlap. We speak of our faith not simply to talk about ourselves. We want to bear witness to what God has done and is doing in our lives. We share faith in this way in the hope that hearers may become interested in our story so that they in turn may see more of God through us.

Testimonies may be public, but because their primary location is within the believing community we must be careful not to transplant the precise *form* of a testimony as used in church to a broader social context. Christians' stories can, of course, be persuasive to those beyond the church. We simply need to be sensitive to discerning when the context for telling is right. The salutary reminder to 'use words if you have to' when being evangelistic is a reminder that testimonies in the form we have been exploring in this chapter may not be the best way to share faith in everyday life. We may need different ways of bearing witness. It is an odd thought that Jesus could be disrespected by being spoken about too much, but it is true. *We* may wish to talk about him in order to offer our testimony, but when people have no desire to listen, and the context for such a testimony is not right, then our witnessing has to take a different shape. Evangelism has to be wordless at times, even if at other times words are just what are needed.

Admittedly, sometimes the avoidance of words becomes a reluctance to bear witness. We need to be challenged here. Close friends that we trust can take us to task: 'Why are you so cagey about your faith? Why don't you just talk as naturally about what you believe God to be doing in your life as you do about the music you like?' But we also have to accept that sometimes it's not possible or easy to use words. Readers will have their own examples of employment situations where speaking openly about one's religious convictions is not possible. Again, then, we are faced with a distinction between evangelism (faith-sharing, not necessarily using words) and testimony (an account of our personal Christian experience).

Our stories, God's story

We pick up finally in this chapter one further insight from Lillian Daniel: 'Testimony seems to have no beginning or end, no alpha or omega. After we tell God's story, it tells us, and then we have a new story to tell. The stories shape the community, and the community responds with new stories. But both the telling and the hearing have the power to transform'.[4] Our testimonies are not fixed stories. Christian faith is a living thing, woven into our daily lives, so we keep on adding to, or adjusting, our testimony. Even if we have some fixed points there will be other 'new life' experiences around and in addition to those which make up the story of our Christian life. The way in which we arrive at our testimony will be the result of our placing our own experiences within the story of God.

POINT OF CONNECTION

'The LORD bless you and keep you; the LORD make his face to shine upon you and be gracious to you; the LORD lift up his countenance upon you and give you peace.' (Exodus 6:24-26)

This is often simply called 'the Blessing' in Christian worship. It draws upon this blessing by God, of Aaron and his sons, by Moses. In other words, tongue-tied Moses blesses Aaron. We could, then, as testimony-givers, share in Aaron's experience!

PRAYER
Living Lord
Whether or not I have the words to express how
I am thankful that you are in my life.
In your good time
help me find a way to show to others
what it means to be your follower
in and through the ups and downs of life.
In Christ you are present with me,
and your Spirit will help me find a way.

Chapter 5

HEARING STORIES: LISTENING FOR THE UNTOLD

Some stories are buried deeply and are either not told or not heard. Acknowledging this, Barbara explores hidden narratives, the place of 'unstory' and the need to listen differently.

We are all aware of the many untold stories and lasting silences we negotiate in our lives. Like icebergs, narratives come to the surface from a deep underground source and what we see on the surface is usually much less than half the story. Everyone has hidden parts of their lives, things that we would prefer not to talk about, stories that have never found words. For a number of years now I have engaged with the stories of people who have experienced abuse, and I want to share some of the insights that I have learned along the way. I think that their wisdom is helpful to everyone who is struggling with untold stories and also can help the Church to be a place that attends more deeply to silence and listening. I believe that understanding how to listen well is as significant to mission as our ability to give accounts of our faith through verbal testimonies.

Untold stories

Life narratives can be snapped, they can be fragmented, shattered, pulverised by traumatic experiences. Trauma disrupts the linear discourse of meaning and extreme trauma, especially in early life, can be devastating, both to individuals and communities. A new language is needed and also a new way of listening.

Maybe more than any other generation, we have had to acknowledge the prevalence of childhood abuse. What had previously been a taboo is now common currency in the media, in biography and in drama. The unthinkable has had to be thought and we have had to face our assumptions around human goodness, about sexual integrity and the assumed safety of the church.   Most people are not abused, and most people are not abusers, but abuse has happened and continues to happen. We have been forced to acknowledge it and also that abuse is trauma. It is robbery with violence, the robbery of childhood, but also of much more. It is the robbery of well-being, of a sense of identity and it causes the brain to make strategies that will affect the rest of life.

We are learning much about the human brain. In the case of unthinkable trauma it will disassociate. This means, it will put the conscious self in a different place from what is currently happening. To take an everyday example, none of us would go to the dentist if we really thought about having a high speed drill in our mouths! In order to get our teeth fixed we are not only required to trust the dentist but we also need to lie in the dentist's chair thinking of something else. Hopefully going to the dentist hasn't resulted in our on-going trauma, but maybe if we've been involved in a car crash, we would understand the next level. When I was in my early twenties I was the passenger in a car that lost control on a wet road and, after spinning around a couple of times, ended up on the wrong side of the A1. Although

I was very shaken at the time, I have gone on to learn to drive and thankfully had an accident-free motoring career. Most of the time I am not reliving the accident, however, on wet roads I am still very nervous. I have a residual memory of losing control and nearly being squashed. The only way I can continue to drive is to put the memory of the crash to the back of my mind, away from my current thinking. This is not a conscious action, rather something my brain does for me in order to allow me to get on with my ordinary life.

Take this up another level: for an abused child to grow beyond early trauma, the brain has to do something with the memories. They need to be 'put out of sight' so that 'normal' life can proceed. There may not even be a memory that something has been forgotten. However, a 'trigger' might cause flashbacks to surface. These may make little sense, the memory of a smell or a fear of having a photo taken, and in some cases, there can be absences where people can give no account of missing lengths of time. In order to function at all most traumatic memories need to be put out of sight, but if they are triggered what seems to surface is apparent non-sense.

POINT OF CONNECTION

I wonder if there are stories you have never told, or only told in part? Are there people around you where you think, 'There's more to this story than meets the eye!'? What might help us tell something of this story or hear more of another person's story? Maybe we could make space for someone by deliberately going for a walk with them or sitting together over a cup of coffee? Maybe we could find somebody who has time to listen to us – either a professional or a good friend?

POINT OF REFLECTION

Nelly and Gladys had sat in neighbouring pews in the same church every Sunday for the past fifty years. It was only when the relative newcomer, Sarah, told them that her first grandchild had been stillborn that the two old women disclosed to each other that they too had lost babies at birth. They were amazed that they had this experience in common but had never shared it before. I wonder how we can share important life stories sooner rather than later?

Unstory

Sometimes what lies below sea-level in the story iceberg is a narrative that not only has never been told but the words haven't got any shape at all; they are a hazy mix of half-memory and sensation.

In her book *The Incredible Woman*, Riet Bons-Storm advocates the term 'unstory.'[1] Joan Laird calls it 'the story that is not there.'[2]

> In unstory a woman cannot give any meaning to her experiences that correspond with her developing self-narrative. Articulating her experience entails acknowledging feelings of pain or shame that she attaches to her story: to do so would cause unbearable incongruence.

So 'unstory' is not simply a secret untold story, but rather a narrative that has no form. What Bons-Storm describes as incongruence is lived out as a disruption to self and may often be experienced by the observer as chaotic or nonsensical behaviour. Of course, such disruption can lead to mental health crises, unexplained physical symptoms or breakdown as the memories 'leak' from their safe place and begin to impact on everyday life. To the observer this behaviour may be odd or irrational, like running away when somebody wants to take a photo, or being frightened of curtains. It may be that the person themselves can't give any rational explanation of their fear because they have not yet accessed the experience that caused the initial trauma.

> The silencing of unstories lies somewhere between imposed and chosen silence. However any interpretation within chosen silence is only understandable in as far as this is preferential to facing the incongruence that would become apparent if a woman were not to choose to be silent: this is likely to occur unconsciously.[3]

As we explore the nature of story we also need to be asking 'What is the unstory? What lies within the silences that surround us and how do we hear incoherent or incongruent narratives that cannot yet, or may never be, expressed in words?'

I would like to point out three things before I go on to explore these questions. Firstly, about terminology. Whilst some people who have experienced trauma would want to describe themselves as 'survivors' or 'victims', I acknowledge that many want to resist these labels. After all, we should not be defined by the actions of someone else, but should claim our own identity in ways that are life-enhancing for us. In the report *Time for Action* it was advocated that we should simply refer to 'people who have experienced abuse'.[4] As you can see I am favouring the word 'trauma' as it puts these experiences into a framework that de-mystifies. The word 'abuse' itself can indicate a number of things, and is also experienced differently by different individuals. It might be helpful to note that the word 'sur -vivre' comes from the French 'to live above', so survivors are not simply victims but rather people who are learning to live over and above their experiences.

Secondly, I don't want to assume that 'survivors' or 'people who have experienced abuse' are somehow other than us. Indeed, you may be reading this with just such experiences in your life. We can safely say that within any gathering of eight or more people there will be at least one (and probably more) people who have experienced trauma or abuse in their lives. This includes every church gathering we attend and everybody that reads this book.

Thirdly, whilst Bons-Storm and many other authors particularly reference the experience of women, it is important to remember that some men have also experienced abuse and whilst I will probably continue to refer to survivors as 'she' this is not intended to exclude anyone.

Having made these points we can now move on to acknowledging 'unstory' and incongruent narratives.

Human story is a mystery and as such is sacred. We hold memories and experiences in deep wells of unknowing, only sharing what we dare, keeping many things to ourselves. As such, we are always surrounded by silences, those that others choose to keep unspoken, and those that are too difficult for words. To respect another's silence is therefore a holy thing.

By the very nature of abuse an individual has been silenced by a fear instilled by the abuser. Such silencing can be deeply debilitating and disruptive to human flourishing. So, how can we respect silence whilst also allowing the possibility of 'hearing into speech'? (Nelle Morton)

Maybe the answer lies in the ability to know that silence is not without content. Silence is the crucible within which the human story is continually formed, re-formed and transformed. By this I mean that silence isn't nothing, but rather an environment in which stories are shaped and ultimately make sense. To wait with others in silence is a subversive act. It is an act of resistance to the dominant narratives that can rob us of words. To be with others in shared silence gives permission for the unstory to exist, even if it is never spoken. Waiting fearlessly with others in silence is in itself a sacred act. There is also wisdom in silence. Once the outer story-telling self is quietened, there is the possibility for the unknown, hidden inner self to emerge. Silence can surprise us and enlarge our understanding, even if this mystery is beyond words.

POINT OF CONNECTION

Silence can be comfortable and uncomfortable, awkward or fruitful. I wonder when we last removed the earphones, unplugged the TV, turned off the car radio and listened out for something different happening?

POINT OF REFLECTION

After Maureen's daughter died, Derek went round to sit with her for a while. He was really anxious that he wouldn't know what to say so he decided that he would let Maureen do the talking. The two of them sat in complete silence for about twenty minutes, after which Maureen wiped her eyes. Derek felt he had been fairly useless but they had a cup of tea and discussed Maureen's garden. When it was time to leave, Maureen gave Derek a hug and thanked him for listening. Can you think of times when you have been lost for words but your silence has been really useful to someone else?

We need to listen differently

Our society, and indeed our Churches, favour the most articulate. That is, those who can express themselves through words, either spoken or written. Sometimes, it just favours the verbose! But our faith is one in which the last are favoured over the first, the poor over the rich and the marginalised over the powerful, albeit we have often squandered these core values and favoured the dominant narratives of power. Yet we are still called to return to the unstory, to read between the lines of our cultural discourse and to listen out for what is not being said. This is gospel.

I believe this is best done by 'listening differently', through an open-ness to creativity, imagination and play. Of course, therapists know this well enough, often enabling clients to explore story using drawing, writing or role play. We also know that the most profound stories are shared on the church walk, or sitting side by side in a car on the way to a meeting. I believe we need an intentional desire to make listening part of our shared life and find opportunities to be together in ways that give space for such listening to happen. When we fall into step together then we can open up alternative spaces for stories to take shape. This is not an invitation to pry, but rather to pause for long enough for deeper truths to emerge and be held. It's not easy, but it is possible. It is the church's mission to be a listening place, and it is our mission to hold as sacred those things that are known only to God.

We should not underestimate this potential. Where else in our society can people be heard without being a 'client' or 'measurable outcome'? Church communities, if they can stop being busy for long enough(!), do have the possibility of listening differently, of holding uncomfortable truths and disruptive stories. After all, isn't that what grace is about? And if we are serious about holding this open space, where people are able to come in their incompleteness, I also believe the church will grow. As one wise person once said, 'Don't just do something, stand there!'

There are a few reminders here though.

When stories do begin to emerge, we fear that we might not be able to listen well enough for long enough. People who have been abused will often 'try out' a story on somebody who appears to be trustworthy. This will most likely come in fragmented form and might not seem believable to the listener. It might come at an inconvenient time, or catch us off guard. It is important, even if the story seems incredible, to receive it. If we need help to hear it, then we must find someone to help us, because the opportunity might not come again. If we are the one chosen to listen, then we can find somebody to share with (without breaking confidentiality) so that we do not re-abuse by not listening well, or cause harm to ourselves. And, the keeping of appropriate boundaries is always the responsibility of the one who listens.

We need to know our limitations. Sometimes untold stories are too hard for us to bear as individuals, there is no shame in helping someone find long-term professional help if that is required. But there's no need to panic either; remember there is great wisdom held in the emerging story. A 'survivor' is not a hapless victim but a resourceful human being who has been through much more than we can ever imagine. They are stronger than we think, so listening, while it might be hard for us, is nothing compared to their remembering the story.

We must resist rushing to theological conclusions. We all hope for happy endings and can come up with some religious truisms to try to circumnavigate the painful journey of encountering the 'unstory'. 'Forgive and forget', 'Time to move on', 'Least said soonest mended' and other shortcuts should be banished from our religious vocabulary. We need to be care-full listeners, not experts. We are simply being asked to hold these painful experiences alongside the transformative love of God. God is not going to fix everything, we know this through the death and crucifixion of Jesus, resurrection does not happen without crucifixion, but mysteriously God is present. Hearing the unstory requires us to re-examine our theologies of suffering, providence and forgiveness and be prepared to read Scripture differently. There are no religious shortcuts to discovering who we are becoming.

Those sacred unstories that are held in the silences of people's hearts, are holy ground. They are the place where life can overcome the deathly cycles of abuse and violence, as such they speak out of deepest anguish with exquisite hope. This is where a new story can emerge, a story of transformative grace. Whether told or untold, these stories struggling to find words are the means by which the hidden self is discovered and more authentic and complex self-narratives can transform our understanding, and help us articulate the complexity and richness of our shared human identities.

POINT OF CONNECTION

What really unhelpful comments have been made to you when you wanted to share something? What helped?

POINT OF REFLECTION

All Mary's family could tell the vicar about her life was that she had liked knitting and that she 'suffered with her nerves', which didn't give much scope for a funeral address. It was only in the vestry before the service, when she asked the church member on duty what 'suffering with her nerves' actually meant that the vicar heard that Mary's father had been a drunk and violent man who had intimidated all the family and abused Mary. She was still processing this information when she walked into church in front of the coffin and faced the family in the front row. It was now necessary to indicate that she knew that Mary's life had been challenging, without disclosing what she knew about the family. She gave space in the eulogy for people to quietly reflect on their own memories rather than simply trying to fill up the space with stories about knitting.

PRAYER

In the speaking and in the spaces
In the unknowing and in the silences
In the things untold or buried
Bring wisdom, Holy Spirit
Bring time, Creator
Bring the Word, beyond words

Chapter 6

JESUS STORIES: ENGAGING WITH THE GOSPELS

Clive looks specifically in this chapter at the role the Gospels play in Christian practice. They are stories themselves, and contain stories. They introduce us to Jesus but also provide materials in relation to which we see our faith developed and honed.

It might seem baffling at first glance as to why the earliest Christians would include four different versions of the Jesus story in their scriptures. Isn't this asking for trouble? If you're trying to put together some kind of norm, or standard, or set of parameters according to which the very varied new Christian communities might be 'reined in' a bit or 'kept in check', then it is not obvious that the best way of doing this is to include four different accounts of the life of the founding figure. It may not suggest that anyone's version of the Jesus story is as good as anyone else's, but it immediately indicates that even orthodox Christianity is not claiming that there is only one Jesus story to be told.

Of course, Jesus made things messy for his immediate

followers. As far as we know, he didn't write anything down. His style was to speak. In the absence of recording devices it was up to others to scribble down what they thought he said, and things were then dependent on whether people grasped what he meant, even whilst they may have heard what he said. The scene from the film *Monty Python's Life of Brian* where those at the back of the crowd listening to the Sermon on the Mount think Jesus said 'blessed are the cheese-makers' is a good joke. ('Well, obviously, it's not meant to be taken literally. It refers to any manufacturers of dairy products', says one hearer in the film.) We are also reminded what we are dealing with when oral culture is the main context in which people pass on traditions. Mishearings, poor memories, different versions of what was and wasn't said, diverse selections of what is deemed important, and multiple, different interpretations of words that are passed on start appearing. Oral culture is living and lively. It can also lead – for good and ill – to less precision than written culture, though we must not underestimate the skill in remembering which good story-tellers have. Think of comedians today who can always improvise and respond to hecklers, so their performances may rarely be exactly the same. But the sheer skill in delivery of similar material night after night shows how good story-telling can work. They learn, and know, their material well. Their timing is impeccable. They know how to 'work a crowd'. They know where the laughs will come.

It is not in the least surprising that Jesus chose not to write. It is also possible he was not even able to. But the emphasis he put on relationships, their quality, and the kind of relationships that would be needed in the Realm/Kingdom of God meant that he would always want to *speak*, and speak *to and with* people. The significance of oral tradition in early Christianity goes beyond the mere fact that most people could not write. It helps us see something about how important oral and aural interactions were, and are, for faith. *In digital, screen-dominated times, this is a telling and challenging observation.* We must not underplay the continuing significance of embodied communication, person to person, happening in the same time and space.

What *is* a Gospel?

'Gospel' has two meanings. First, it means 'good news' (glad tidings). When the story of Jesus is told, it has to be presented in such a way that it is going to have a chance of being heard positively and transformatively by the hearer or reader. Second, a Gospel is a written version of the Jesus story. It is a literary form that contains such a good news story. Sometimes we can mistakenly think that Gospels are life-stories. They are life-stories only in a limited sense. We must not think of them as 'biographies' in first-century terms, or in twenty-first century terms. They are not carefully-researched scholarly accounts of Jesus' life, where all the facts have been double-checked. Nor are they 'hagiographies' – stories which 'big someone up' and miss out the unpleasant bits of their life-story. Even the Gospels acknowledge that there are tricky elements in Jesus's story (e.g. Matthew 15:21-28, Mark 7:21-30) and they don't leave these bits out.

Are Gospels 'testimonies'? They aren't in any straightforward sense. For they are not accounts of the lives of people *other than* Jesus. The accounts of Jesus are, however, tangled up with testimony, because the Jesus story is told, in four different ways, in a way which reflects the impact of Jesus on his followers, during his own lifetime and later. They can, then, present the story of Jesus *as* Good News, in the *form* of a Gospel, *because* they have witnessed Jesus's transformative impact on their lives. They can tell these stories, because they have allowed their own life-stories to get tangled up with Jesus's story.

The Gospels are texts. Even if we receive them as examples of 'frozen words' – capturing a segment of the lively oral culture in which Jesus and his first followers lived, worked, taught and performed – it was essential for those of us who follow later that these stories were put down on paper, papyrus, parchment and scrolls. The earliest followers had to work out how they would be able to tell others about Jesus beyond the story-telling culture of the immediate Palestinian setting in which Jesus acted and spoke. Receiving the texts now, as sections of an authoritative set of scriptures, their liveliness can easily be lost. Our job, all the time, is to make them live again – as stories we pass on, but also as stories we inhabit ourselves, stories that shape who we are. We have to tell them (make them oral again), and tell other stories like them. But four – why do we have four?

There are lots of theories about why we have four particularly – as opposed to three, six or seven, say. We don't need to go into that here. What we do need to do is take very seriously the fact that there is more than one. Oral culture delivered lots of stories. But written culture did not then close down the options and produce a single Jesus story. Even when tough choices had to be made about what would be in the New Testament, four different texts remained in place. Simply because something was called a Gospel didn't mean it would qualify. The Gospels of Thomas and Peter and the Infancy Gospel of James didn't make it, for example. But why keep a number of them?

We must be careful not to make the assumption that at a specific time and place a number of learned scholars or church-leaders sat down with a lot of texts and sifted through them weighing up their various merits. That is not how the New Testament came about. Groupings of texts were made (different collections of Paul's letters, for instance). Practical use and usefulness, support by particular church-leaders, assumed association with apostles (Mark was often linked with Peter, for example) were some of the reasons why texts became established as reliable. Even so, it would have been possible to say: 'One should be enough, surely! It will save us all a lot of bother later.' But that didn't happen. There are four, irreducibly four. Christianity carries with it a flexibility and a diversity for which we can simply thank God.

But what does this mean for us now, in practice? What do we do with four accounts of Jesus's life?

POINT OF REFLECTION
Which particular Gospel do you in practice refer to most? (Why?) Which one has influenced you the most in the particular version of Christian faith that you hold? (Why?)

Are your answers to the two previous questions the same? (And if not, why do you think that is?)

One Jesus, four gospels, one very big Christ – but how many stories?

Despite the multiple accounts, there was only one Jesus of Nazareth. In claiming that this Jesus was the Christ (the Messiah), Jesus' early followers were identifying him as the decisive figure in human history, the 'One who is to come', the one who signals the end of time. They placed him within the story of Israel, the story of Messianic expectation, the story of the coming Realm/Kingdom of God. In other words, Jesus offered, by his words and actions, ways for his followers to make sense of what he was about and who he was. How explicit he was about all this, scholars will go on debating.

Jesus' followers could, though – because they 'knew the story' – go on interpreting who Jesus was and what he stood for, and keep on pinpointing how and where God in Christ (in Jesus-like ways) was active in the world. They would be helped by God's Spirit in this task of discernment.

In the process, they would inevitably tell the story of Jesus in fresh and different ways. As they told it, they would start reflecting later concerns as they cropped up. This 'filling out' of the story would start very early. Matthew, Mark, Luke and John all represent examples of re-telling the Jesus story in new situations, beyond the time of the life of Jesus of Nazareth. They are therefore 'stories about Jesus' (the historical figure), but at the same time stories about how this Jesus has had an impact upon, and provided meaning and purpose for, a later group of Jesus' followers. We shall remind ourselves about how these four Gospels take shape, and what their emphases are, in the next section. First, we need to note something of what is happening both within the New Testament and beyond when the story of Jesus is told.

As we keep on discovering in relation to so many of the stories which we as Christians tell, we are not just providing historical facts. When we tell the story of Jesus we are linking back to the historical figure of Jesus. But we are also saying something about God. The claim that God was in, and with, Jesus in a unique way affects how the story is told. We are saying something about ourselves too: in wanting to tell Jesus-stories we are suggesting how and why he has had an impact upon us, folding into our tale implicitly or explicitly aspects of the kind of faith in him we hold. We are indicating that we count ourselves as 'in Christ'. In being a follower of Jesus we are signalling that we belong with other followers too. So we can accept that others may be followers of Jesus in different ways from us. At its simplest, then, this is why different Gospels exist, and why so many different faith stories can be told: people go on telling their own life-stories in relation to the stories of Jesus, and each affects the other.

Believing that God really was and is at work in Jesus the Christ brings the stories to life. Our engagement with Jesus stories, our re-telling of them, and our attempts to live in relation to them celebrates all that continues in the name of Christ and the fact that the presence of Christ persists. When as Christians we talk about Jesus we are never just talking about Jesus, but we have to be careful. If we are also talking about ourselves, we need to ensure we are not *just* talking about ourselves. Otherwise we might be talking about ourselves instead of talking about Jesus.

There can, then, remain a 'oneness in Christ' beneath, above, around and within all the different Jesus stories which are told. The range and variety of Jesus stories will nevertheless find some kind of unity, despite the difference. Christ is a big tent. How, though, does the diversity of Jesus stories, and the fact that those stories mix with the stories of the tellers (past tellers, and present tellers), take effect?

Nikki, Matthew, Jack, Mark, Tammy, Luke, Ariko and John

Rather than start with the Gospels themselves, let's start the other way round. Think of four people:

Nikki likes Matthew's Gospel. It seems to be particularly interested in getting a message of righteousness across. People know what they've got to do, when they read or hear Matthew. But as well as making the message clear, there's an emphasis on *teaching* the message. Perhaps we have to be teachers like Jesus. (Nikki's a teacher herself.) Perhaps that's what Matthew is emphasizing. She was even made aware that Matthew may have structured his whole Gospel like the Pentateuch – the first five books of the Old Testament – as if to say: Jesus offers a new kind of Law. And perhaps that's why

Matthew seems very keen indeed to slot Jesus into Jewish tradition, pointing out where Jesus appears to fit in with, and develop, what the whole Jewish tradition, prophets and all, was about.

Jack likes Mark's rough-and-readiness. It was a while before someone pointed out to him that the word 'immediately' appears quite a lot in the Gospel (27 times, to be precise), but it makes sense: there's a lot of urgency in Mark which makes the Jesus portrayed there a compelling figure. There's no time to lose! Get on with the job of welcoming the Kingdom of God! Preach it! Live it! Jack likes that, because his own life was turned round quite dramatically after a tough time in his twenties. He recognises how important and urgent it can prove to discover what the figure of Jesus, and all that Jesus stands for, can mean for those who hear a story like Mark's.

Tammy likes the shepherds very much, and that's why she likes Luke. She works on a farm, but it's not the countryside aspect of the shepherds' story which grabs her. She likes Luke because Luke seems to 'get' outsiders: those whom society shoves to the edges. She has long felt that Jesus' siding with outsiders has to be the key through which all else about God is understood and told. We can't all be outsiders, but our stories (and the church's stories) have to do more than just keep in with outsider perspectives. That's what Tammy sees in Luke. Her Jesus is 'the friend of sinners' in a big way.

Ariko is a bit of a mystic. That's not in a 'look at me, I'm different' kind of way. It's simply that he feels things deeply and carries with him a strong spiritual sensibility. All the time he believes and senses that he is part of something bigger, and that he lives his life within the great, overarching spiritual presence of God. He wonders whether that's why he likes the Gospel of John so much. The Jesus of the Fourth Gospel behaves, and comes over to the reader or hearer, rather differently from the first three Gospels. There is more of an account here of a Jesus with a very developed inner life, and a strong, deep sense of oneness with God, his Father. If we're to 'be like Jesus' then, for Ariko, this isn't just about following the actions and doing good deeds. It has to include latching onto Jesus' spirituality, and that's what he sees very clearly in John's Gospel.

POINT OF CONNECTION
Think back to your answers to the 'Point of Reflection' questions' above. What do your answers look like now, having just heard those four accounts? Did any of the accounts of Nikki, Jack, Tammy and Ariko strike chords with you, or make your reconsider your earlier answers?

There is a drier version of those personal responses to the four canonical Gospels. Matthew is 'the Teacher's Gospel'. Mark is 'the Activist's Gospel'. Luke is the 'Social Reformer's Gospel'. John's is 'the Mystic's Gospel'. These are oversimplifications, but as summaries, they indicate clear tendencies or emphases of the four texts.

What, though, are we to do with these differences? In the same way that the narratives of Jesus' birth are meshed together – so that Magi (from Matthew) and Shepherds (from Luke) are put together into a single story – are we simply to mesh all the Evangelists' accounts into a single Jesus story?

We shouldn't for three reasons. First, it's not even possible. In the same way that different accounts of any event will have differences and not be easily reconcilable, so also we shouldn't attempt to flatten or stifle what are lively witnesses to who Jesus was. Stifling these accounts by squelching them together fails to do the accounts justice as creatively-constructed Gospels in their own right. Second, trying to force them into a single story would have a negative impact on our understanding and presentation of what the ongoing presence of God in Christ in the world amounts to *now*. By inheriting multiple voices and multiple accounts, we see that the witness to Jesus the Christ has to be diverse. The 'one very big Christ' we referred to earlier demands breadth and diversity. Jesus helps us see the sheer range and depth of who God connects with and what God wants to do with and for the world. Third, therefore, by leaving the different accounts alongside each other, we allow the single story of Jesus (and thus the ongoing story of Jesus as the Christ) to be accessed by a broader range of types of follower. Ariko, Tammy, Jack and Nikki can all find their own way to Jesus, and relate to his ongoing story in the present, because they are offered different points of access. The different accounts of the character, personality and purpose of Jesus enables followers with different character and personality types to find a point of connection.

We could perhaps say, then, that it doesn't matter that there are four Gospels in the New Testament. That's too defensive. It's better to say that it's a strength that there are four Gospels. More people can find out who God is, in and through the person of Jesus, as portrayed in the multiple ways the New Testament offers that Jesus to us.

PRAYER

Ever-present Christ, again and again
I have said, like Mary Magdalene,
'They have taken away my Lord,
and I do not know where they have laid
him.'
I have felt abandoned,
yet you have always kept looking for me,
and found me.
Every time, I know that what I have lost is
not you,
but only my idea of who you are,
an image I have made to keep hold of what
I have found,
and to be my security, within my own
control.
I shall go on making images, O Lord,
better than the last.
That next image will fade too,
and all successive images.
But you will remain
beyond all my images
beyond all images.'

Chapter 7

SHARING STORIES: LIVING BETWEEN FAITHS

In this chapter, Barbara tells the story of one particular project and the way in which it enables interfaith dialogue to happen at lots of different levels. She shares the parameters of good dialogue but also moves into and embraces complexity in the stories that we tell.

In 2017, the Touchstone project, a Methodist interfaith initiative in the centre of Bradford West Yorkshire, went into partnership with the British Foreign and Commonwealth Office in a project called Weaving Women's Wisdom. This unlikely alliance happened because the Foreign Office was looking at ways to improve the stories told about Pakistan and Pakistanis in British culture. Those employed by the Foreign Office, however, were not practitioners at a local level, neither were they experts in the intricacies of interfaith dialogue 'on the ground', so they needed help to connect with local communities in order to deliver their objectives. Touchstone, a grassroots organisation was very skilled in just that; they had been working at local level for more than 30 years, but did not have the international reach or the financing of a Government body. Both sides took the risk of working together.

Touchstone were concerned that what they delivered in neighbourhoods was not always taken seriously at national level. Touchstone's work is primarily with women in a majority Pakistani heritage community, yet often it was dismissed as 'craft groups with women' rather than changing policy from the bottom up. On the national stage inter-religious dialogue often involved faith leaders discussing policy or responding to incidents. This high profile coverage tended to involve prominent leaders giving voice to policy issues - and they were usually men.

Touchstone knew from experience that to make good policy required engaging with the complexity and nuance of experience in local communities. Also, Touchstone staff were not threatened by talking about faith or by listening to people of other faiths. Touchstone could offer their faith literacy to this work and enable a multiplicity of voices to emerge. To really improve the profile of different ethnic groups in British society needed to give space to voices where faith and identity were intertwined in complex ways. To this end they needed to bring all their wisdom and experience of creative dialogue.

The intention of the project was relatively simple. Groups of women were asked to gather and reflect on four questions. These questions were centred around the theme of 'Wisdom' which is common to all faith traditions. Theology was central for the exchange, but it was not for the academy or for recognised church leaders, rather for those whose voices are rarely heard in the public square. The project wanted to start from the common ground that the participants shared and give access to talking around their theology in ways that enabled a broad and accepting environment. The four questions were these:

- What is the wisest piece of advice you have ever been given?
- Who is/was the wisest woman in your life?
- Who are the wise women in your faith tradition?
- What is the difference between wisdom and knowledge?

The women were encouraged to gather over a few weeks and to let the conversation happen. They were also given a piece of rug canvas and some wool, cloth and other resources on which to make a design that reflected their conversation. There were 20 groups across the UK and some in Pakistan; participants were Christian, Muslim, Buddhist, Pagan, Hindu and Sikh.

POINT OF CONNECTION
Wisdom is a common thread to all faith traditions, I wonder how you would answer the questions above and how your answers might be different from those of the people around you?

POINT OF REFLECTION
One of the rugs had the words 'For Just Such a Time as This' and was made by a small group of Christian and Muslim friends. The words come from the Book of Esther, found in both Christian and Jewish Scriptures (Esther 4:14). I wonder what you could glean from reading this story together with people of different faith and what wisdom you might be called to speak together for just such a time?

What is dialogue and how can it lead to story telling?

The World Council of Churches and the Vatican had over time suggested four ways in which effective interfaith dialogue occurs. These can be summarised as:

1. The Dialogue of Life – in which people of different faiths and spiritual traditions strive to live in an open and neighbourly spirit – includes socialising and hospitality

2. The Dialogue of Action – in which people of spiritual commitment and faith collaborate with others in building a just society – includes service and working for justice

3. The Dialogue of Religious Experience – in which people steeped in their spiritual traditions share their ways of searching for God or the Absolute – includes prayer, worship, celebration.

4. The Dialogue of Theological Exchange – in which specialists seek to deepen their understanding of other spiritual heritages.[1]

Dialogue is essentially an act of storytelling, one in which there is an equal exchange of listening and speaking. Touchstone wanted to demonstrate that these WCC categories were not mutually exclusive and that it was possible to talk about experience, text and theology while at the same time being engaged in everyday life and common activity. It was with this in mind that the Weaving Women's Wisdom project was launched. Touchstone also had in mind the World Council of Churches guidelines for dialogue. They knew that dialogue must be a process of mutual empowerment, not a negotiation between parties who have conflicting interests and claims. Also that in dialogue we are invited to grow in faith, not strive to undermine or change the faith of another, that we are called together to affirm hope and to create human communities of justice and peace, to nurture good relations and build friendships so that mutual respect and self-understanding can flourish. This needs to happen in an atmosphere of acceptance and honesty in which the integrity of an individual's religion can be honoured. This should be as open and inclusive as possible.

Ultimately dialogue is about listening and learning, both to each other and to our shared context, bearing in mind historical experience, economic background and political ideologies. It should be a cooperative and collaborative activity and based on a shared sense of mutuality and justice.

In naming this need we also need to name our fears. Fear of being overwhelmed, of being thought stupid, of being racist or of losing sight of our own precious beliefs as we engage with others. There is work to be done to increase appropriate confidence in faith communities so we are robust enough to face our fears and to risk making relationships with people who are profoundly different from ourselves. It is a call to be courageous amongst the dominant narratives of terrorism, extremism, colonialism and capitalism to be able to articulate what difference faith means to us and those around us. One Muslim woman said in a Touchstone group that it was the first time she had been given safe space to give a positive account of her faith, mostly people wanted simply to quiz her about her hijab or imply negative things about Islam, but she wanted to say that her faith brought enlightenment to her life and had a positive influence on her well-being.

Being prepared to live with complex interfaith narratives is counter-cultural. Many people like simple stories, explanations of why things are as they are, why people behave as they do. But through Touchstone's interfaith encounters it is possible to realise that we are both individual and a product of our cultural mores and religious beliefs.

Nobody can speak 'for' Muslims just as nobody can speak on behalf of all Christians. Indeed intra-faith dialogue is often more tortuous than conversations across faiths. In intra-faith dialogue we are asked to talk with people of our own faith who hold different theological persuasions. There is possibly a bigger chasm between Pentecostal Christians and Quakers than between Quakers and Sufi Muslims. Interfaith conversation thus challenges us to face our own diversity as well as engaging beyond the stereotypes we have of others. And also to see how our stories have converged and diverged through history as we have battled for territory and power.

With an eye to these guidelines and fears, Touchstone staff acted as facilitators within the groups, not attending every session but being willing to drop by to aid the process of conversation and to help with practical skills. Facilitating this framework for creative dialogue ensured that everyone in the group had a voice and that good relationships were forming around the common task. They soon found that the women were happily engaging in the activity and also with profound sharing around their faith journeys. Comparisons were made between Biblical and Q'ranic figures, a Pagan and a Buddhist got talking about peacebuilding and a group of young women were meeting in their school dinner time to talk together and finish the rug. The stories told were rich and multi-layered.

POINT OF CONNECTION
What makes safe space for dialogue and what are the challenges in the WCC guidelines? Do we have any good examples of creative dialogue and what stories emerged when you overcame your fear?

POINT OF REFLECTION

We spend so much time, staring at the sky, hoping God will notice us through some heavenly binoculars. But, like Hagar, we need to believe in the living water, deep down in the cracked, parched earth under our feet. When we are most vulnerable and lost, God hands us a spade.

We are called to dig deep , to shovel to hunker down, to sift and claw the soiled, scarred earth, until even in the spoil heap of our own bewildering pain we uncover some small surprising thing, some essential, precious, lovely pearl that bears our true name, our glorious fragile strength.

Complexity and joy

Many of the rugs communicated deeply personal and painful stories. One group of women included asylum seekers who had recently arrived in the UK having fled Syria and North Africa. Although their English was fairly limited, the rug gave them the ability to tell their refugee stories. To the right of the rug was a barren tree in a desert landscape. In the central area, blue wool denoted the ocean with felt boats attached. Each boat had individual buttons sewn into it, as each woman described her journey. Some wept as they described parting from family, some having to decide which child to bring and which to leave behind. To the left of the rug, a luxuriant apple tree denoting the land of plenty to which they had dreamed of coming. Like the script of their countries of origin the rug 'read' from right to left.

In this, and many of the projects that Touchstone has

engaged with, there has been a rich depth of story-telling that has moved the encounter to a new level and to a deeper engagement. In one group a Pakistani Christian and an Indian Christian had a long conversation about Partition. A Pakistani Christian and a Pakistani heritage Bradfordian Muslim talked about interfaith tensions in Pakistan. An Indian Hindu and an Indian Christian discussed the politics influenced by the caste system. These multi-layered, complex and nuanced encounters between people of different faith and culture enabled participants to experience rich moments of encounter, to engage with paradox and move beyond stereotypes.

Whilst the rug project was taking place other members of the Touchstone staff were working in conjunction with Churches Together in Britain and Ireland Interfaith Theological Advisory group to revisit the guidelines for interfaith dialogue outlined by the World Council of Churches. The group was anxious that the guidelines should be enhanced by stories of real life experience so that churches and individuals could be encouraged in their own settings. To this end a small booklet *Acting in God's Love* was produced which is a collection of encounters between different faith traditions gathered from practical experience across the UK. The story of the rug making was included in the booklet.[2]

Some of the rugs referred directly to passages of scriptures. One group compared the story of the Woman at the Well, in John's gospel and the pilgrimage of the Haaj made by many Muslims. The person of Hagar was discussed and the differences between the Hebrew Bible/ Old Testament account and the Q'ran. This rug reflected the importance of water in holy narratives and also in everyday life, especially enabling the women to talk about times at which they shed tears.

The Weaving Women's Wisdom rugs were gathered

into an exhibition which was launched in Bradford Town Hall with representatives of the Foreign Office in attendance. Since then it has been on tour to various religious and secular venues, including Ripon and Bradford Cathedrals and the Methodist Conference. Most recently it was nominated by a local MP to be exhibited in the Houses of Parliament, thus becoming a topic of conversation amongst those 'in power'. Very recently *Look North*, a local TV news programme for the BBC, featured the Weaving Women's Wisdom as a positive project enabling social cohesion in the region during Interfaith Week. The story is clearly not finished yet!

The term 'interfaith' can be fraught with misunderstanding and difficulties. There are those who think that their religion is the only true path, others who think all religions are basically the same, and all shades in between. Many theologians have described these many positions of inter-religious engagement as inclusivist, pluralist or exclusivist, but we need to move beyond this to engage with the richer and more complex mixture of cultures and beliefs that run through our current social and political landscape. This engagement with complexity is not about who might be on the right side of the line with God, but rather a call into the here and now of our multi-faith and multi-ethnic experience.

In the book *Salvation Means Creation Healed*, Snyder and Scandrett recall us again to the re-integration of the work of the kingdom in the incarnate realities of our times.[3] They remind us of the common thread of shalom, peace, healing that is at the centre of all faith and that is worked out through healthy relationships. Conversations between people of faith are a holy matter, earthed in our shared realities but essentially about the salvation of the earth here and now. And, these conversations need to travel from academy to community, from practice to theory and between politicians and practitioners and back again. It is no longer sufficient to rely on leaders to speak on our behalf, or for community activists alone to engage with matters of social inclusion, but rather a long-term commitment to enabling discourse from the powerless to the powerful and effective listening to multi layered, complex challenges.

Wherever we sit, we ignore engagement with the conversation at our peril. We are living in times which might in some quarters be described as secular, but have never been more influenced by religion. And this need for interfaith conversation is not something limited to multicultural areas, in fact the more mixed parts of the country are probably already involved in discourse of one type or another. But racists move away from mixed areas; probably the place most needing inter-religious dialogue is the English village where somebody from just a few miles away is seen as the enemy! The need to see and converse with 'the other', wherever we live, is crucial to building peaceful communities wherever we are, and a primary calling to people of faith. This need neither diminish our own faith nor necessarily convert another person to our point of view; rather it will add subtlety and complexity to our relationships, enabling new insights into our own traditions whilst learning about another's.

The Weaving Women's Wisdom project has been an extraordinary example of interfaith work that has engaged both locally and nationally, privately and publicly, in this country and in Pakistan. There has been learning on all sides, and also a lot of laughter. But of course, such work is also vulnerable and fragile. Heightening tension in Pakistan, the increased racism that has resulted from Brexit conversations, political uncertainty in the Middle East can all supplant complex narrative held in communities with a rhetoric of oppression. The necessity to continually open the door for the stranger and to live with our fear and uncertainty is at the heart of all our faith traditions, the living of it will be a challenge for years to come. Meanwhile living fearlessly within complex stories is our continuing vocation.

Engaging with stories of faith and between faiths is a rich source of insight. As women engaged with the Weaving Women's Wisdom project they were able to see each other with fresh eyes through the stories that were shared, both personal and from their holy texts. They were also able to hold the points at which narratives diverged with compassion and understanding and found a new story through being together around a shared task. Within this rich complexity of narrative firm friendships were formed, but also a new confidence was found with which to speak into the public sphere. This transformative process has the potential of influencing both personal life and wider policy enabling a much needed broader narrative for multicultural identity. The outcomes of the project have been far reaching, both at a personal and strategic level. The exhibitions, reflection and publications that have emerged during the course of and as a result of the Weaving Women's Wisdom project have enhanced the dialogue of life, action, religious experience and theological exchange in both simple and profound ways and provided a model of good practice to be celebrated and shared.

POINT OF CONNECTION

Where in our lives has being courageous taken us to form new friendships or discover surprising insights? When have we been tempted to oversimplify our differences?

POINT OF REFLECTION

Bertrand Russell said: 'Fear is the main source of superstition, and one of the main sources of cruelty. To conquer fear is the beginning of wisdom.'

Albert Einstein said: 'Any intelligent fool can make things bigger and more complex, it takes a lot of courage and a touch of genius to take things in the opposite direction.'

Desmond Tutu said: 'Bringing people together is what I call "Ubuntu" which means "I am because we are." Far too often people think of themselves as just individuals separated from one another, whereas you are connected and what you do affects the whole world. When you do well, it spreads out; it is for the whole of humanity.'

Discuss!

PRAYER
May the courage of the Wise One inspire us
the compassion of Jesus lead us
the laughter of the Spirit dance with us
until we discover the simple depths of
friendship
that will change the World.

Chapter 8

CREATING STORIES: BEING CREATIVE

We are creatures who create. We have been created, somehow, mysteriously, amazingly, surprisingly and we are mysterious, amazing and surprising. The question of why and how we have been created is a scientific, philosophical and religious question. The relationship between our creativity and our Creator is one that fascinates us and gives us hope. With respect to this chapter, Barbara comments: 'What I am writing here is "a work in progress" because I am still discovering what it might mean to have been imagined by the source of all life. As you journey with me through this chapter you will be able to hear my thoughts circling, laughing and playing, hold tight!'

Imagining

All creativity begins in the imagination, with a wondering question, and with a connection between otherwise unlinked concepts or thoughts. This might be as simple as threading two distinct colours together on a weaving loom, or as complex as the Theory of Relativity. It is apt to refer to creativity as a 'spark' as if a thought leaps across two as yet unconnected wires, or across a synapse, a leap between what is known and what is unseen, a conversation between the conscious and the subconscious. Creativity quickens in a heartbeat, it is the beginning of a dance, the first tentative word of a story, a notion that causes a smile or the furrowing of a brow. As such it comes from mystery, even though it might result from ideas and forms of the past. It is a call into a new thing, a fresh way of seeing, an exploration in an unknown landscape.

This spark is both immanent and transcendent. It asks questions of form and structure, but also of meaning and time. It comes out of our humanness but is more than our humanness, it is both our calling and our gift. As such, it is a combination of freedom and discipline. The artist, sculptor, writer is both invited to think freely and to explore widely, but also to have the painstaking skill of their craft. The painter must understand perspective as well as abstraction, the storyteller needs to understand narrative form and carve out words, as a sculptor chips at marble. Commonly, the story or painting begins to take on a life of its own. It is as if it 'speaks back' and begins to create the creator. Even the most solitary artist is in a conversation with their work, ploughing the furrows in a field of thought.

This conversation is on-going and never complete, it is a timeless quest. The writer or painter finds absorption in the process of creation, they lose track of time as they wrestle with the subject. They are taken to another world in which the creative process is life itself. They are often difficult to live with! This communication and interconnection between creativity and creation becomes the dance by which each circles the other, pushing towards something as yet undisclosed. There is a final goal, but often it is not satisfactory, the process raises more questions than it answers, there is always a drive to something more, something better, more truthful. But when the creator releases the work and moves on, the object itself begins a different story as people observe it, question it, read it and find their own meaning or relationship within it. Any author or sermon writer knows that our attempts to write are interpreted in a multitude of intended and unintended ways once we release the words and let them land where they will.

This spark between the immanent and the transcendent, takes us to questions beyond subjectivity. The artist, musician or writer is able to imagine worlds beyond physical reality, outside time or the present ordering of the Universe. They can engage with abstraction, in which they are able to take shape and form and see it differently, unconfined by the rules of our perceived reality. They can ask 'What if ...' questions of life and push at the edges of things.

POINT OF CONNECTION
Can you think of a piece of art, music or writing that has made you see life differently?
Where does your imagination play? (For me it's when it suddenly sees the funny side of a serious situation and makes a joke!)

Point of Reflection
The sculptor Rachel Whiteread, took ordinary objects, a bed, a chair, a desk and began to make casts of the spaces underneath things. In her work 'Ghost' she made a cast of a room in a house soon to be demolished. She caused us to ask questions about the things that are no longer there, our parents,

our lost stories, our everyday realities, in ways that explored the space between things rather than the objects themselves.

In the work 'Shibboleth', Doris Salcedo exhibited a crack in the floor of the Turbine Hall, Tate Modern (2007). In this seemingly simple installation the artist explored racial hatred, the distrust of the immigrant, crossing borders, the fissure between the developing and developed world. She invited the viewer to peer down into the crack into what she describes as 'the epicentre of catastrophe.' This ever-widening crack broke open the floor of this iconic space causing people to end up on different sides. Salcedo literally 'broke new ground' and her work is a seemingly political comment, aiming to interpret the world from the perspective of the defeated people. Even though it is now covered, the scar remains below the floor of the Turbine Hall, a continuing if invisible reminder of the dispossessed people of Salcedo's home country of Colombia.

What other artists, writers or musicians have caused you to push at the edge of things or ask 'What if …' questions?

Mystery

Creativity is a conversation with mystery, it is about colour and shape, shadow and form, but it is also about impossibility, surprise, justice, passion and ultimately about truth. As Salcedo shows it is also about facing the void. It is torment. There is not only the tyranny of the empty page, the blank canvas, but also the sight of chaos that can drive creatives demented. There are never sufficient resources or skill to express fully what is perceived by the inner eye. There is always more to be unravelled, always a sense of incompleteness, always a drive to a new edge. Creativity and insanity are close companions.

I wonder then, how we might re-enter the biblical narratives with the eye of the artist or poet. Not just to recognise that there are different forms of writing in the text, but also to discover God as creativity itself? It is not simply that God makes the world in Genesis and then becomes an absentee landlord, but rather that creativity is at the heart of life and faith. The first command to humanity is to be fruitful and multiply, that is to be creative. God's desire is that we imagine more than ourselves, to ask questions of existence, to look beyond the immediate, to let life flourish.

Psalmists didn't simply write songs, but also envisaged a world beyond the torment of the day as their imaginations began dancing on the edge of time and space with a vision of how life could be made new. The Israelites were called out of the drudgery of manufacturing bricks by a man who had dreams and visions and knew how to tell stories to people in power. We discover Jesus the storyteller, drawing pictures of an upside-down kingdom in the dust of political occupation. In the books of Daniel and Revelation we find visions of the abyss, painted with vivid apocalyptic terror and the imaging of a new heaven and new earth described in such detail that it has inspired artists through the centuries. We discover time and eternity rubbing shoulders and the spark of imagination bringing new life to birth, always with a sense of incompleteness, until the Creator calls things back to the source. We are continually offered a blank canvas, a clean page on which to write life's manuscript. The stories of God are worked and reworked, transforming the commonplace in the light and shadow of lived experience. We are encouraged to view life from the edge, changing perspective on the assumptions of power, seeing the gaps and the cracks and the spaces in between. Perceiving the Divine as the creativity that continually brings new vision into being, the Word made flesh.

Creativity is at the heart of God's being. And when we are creative we share in this story, exploring the interface between the imagination and the unknown, dredging meaning out of despair, entering the story of creativity itself by asking questions of its mystery through paint, poetry, sculpture, film, through the multiplicity of the rich materials of the Earth.

POINT OF CONNECTION

There is a primal link between creativity and story. Through our creative energy there is both an exploration of self and a discovery of self in relation to others and to our environment.

Does this ring true to you? What practical consequences flow from your response?

POINT OF REFLECTION

The stories we tell of God's creativity, span all religions. They begin in wonder and attribute God's love for the Earth and its people to his love, desire for flourishing and for life itself.

'In the earliest Hebrew creation stories Yahweh makes himself a clay model of a man and breathes on it to give it life. It is this supreme confidence, this translation of forms, the capacity to recognise in one thing the potential of another and the willingness to let this potential realise itself, is the stamp of creativity and the birthright that Yahweh gives to humans.'[1]

Annie Dillard writes,

'Our life is a faint tracing on the surface of mystery...we must sometimes take a wider view, look at the whole landscape, describe what's going on here. Then we can at least wail the right question into the swaddling band of darkness, or if it comes to that choir the proper praise.'[2]

Where do these quotes resonate with your experience of creativity and creation?

Delight in creative process

We are created beings, and as such we are also creative in our desire to imagine more than ourselves as we ask questions of the material world. Questions about light, about the spaces between things, about the unknown. Through creativity we converse with mystery, with colour, with form. We are surprised by the juxtaposition of things, by texture and textile by life, both seen and unseen. We consistently find within humanity the desire to create, to explore what is around the next corner, to ask questions of the known and the unknown. Our creativity makes us look below the surface of things, to ask questions of the material world, of light, of scale, of edge, of time, of the mystery of life in all its dimensions.

I have realised, far too late in my adult life, that when I am being creative I feel closest to the Creator. That writing or painting or weaving a piece of cloth is not only prayerful but is prayer. That through this embodied activity, I make the connections between my story and the ultimate stories of life itself. I had always thought that my creative ventures were my leisure activities, to be undertaken when I had spare time. Now I see that they are essential to my identity and to my understanding of the work of God within me. They are not simply recreation but re-creation. To be made in God's imagination is a call to imagine the world differently in the light of the stories around me, bringing my creativity alongside the on-going creation of the Earth.

Creativity also brings a new sense of value to the body. Imagination may happen in the brain but the realisation of the vision that the brain has concocted comes through the hands, the eyes, the ears, every part of the body as we learn to interpret that vision in paint or poetry. The sacramental work of making an outer sign of an inner reality. The body is to be honoured differently as it learns new arts, translates feelings through paint, expresses passions through dance. Our creativity gives expression to the Spirit within us. It also enables us to express our fears, anguish and trepidation. It unlocks our faith from our heads and bears witness to the impulse of the eternal questions that burble within us. It transforms our faith journey from cerebral reasoning which many think is favoured by our left brains. Creativity is a whole body thing, involving head and heart enabling our left hands to join in as equals (or right hands for left handed people!). It re-balances our body so that we have permission to doubt, ask questions, explore, adventure and play as well as live by the logic that the rational world favours.

Creativity brings delight, beauty, hope, colour, variety,

subtlety, possibility, joy. It asks questions of time and eternity. It finds meaning in everyday things. There is a quest to it, it is never still. It is the stuff of faith.

So why is church so often dull? Why are we so often spectators in the theatre of worship? How can we move beyond banner making and Messy Church to see that we are called into Divine creativity, not as an activity when the serious things have been accomplished, but as a core vocational engagement with the stories of God? How have we managed so often to lock out creativity and be trapped in the spoken and written word? Of course, words are creative and can paint pictures too but if salvation finds its roots in 'salve' meaning the 'wide open spaces of freedom' then how are we to embody this in a new way that allows our creative souls to sing new songs in the strange landscapes we inhabit using things other than words? How could we make Church a safe place to visualise a new heaven and a new earth, a new politic, environmental flourishing, how can we make it a life-giving place?

LGBTQ communities, people with learning disability, people with mental ill health, children, the politically radical, in fact anyone who doesn't feel comfortable conforming to expected 'norms' are often excluded by the Church and their creativity is lost. Opening the doors to diversity will also open the doors to increased creativity, but there will need to be change. A creative exploration of 'the edges' and an openness to being born again in the imagination of the artist God. As we are called to release faith from being just in our heads and let it be an embodied reality amongst us, we have much to learn from those who explore the world through the arts. But not so that we can simply observe their expertise or alternative interpretations of the things around us, but so that we can be unchained to find the creative God enabling our own creativity. Embodying the questions of identity and meaning in the light of God's love, is surely both vocational and missional.

Creativity also has the potential to transform community as we observe and interpret the world around us with fresh eyes, as we allow the stories of faith to weave in and out of our everyday lives. Why do we have so many bland church fronts, so many word-clogged noticeboards, so many signs telling church users what they are not permitted to do? How can our church buildings reflect the joyous colour, mystery and beauty of the gifts of God?

Here's a simple idea that we tried out at Touchstone. We asked people to take a quick picture of one particular drawer in their house or garage that told something about them. We asked them to send in their snap and we would publish it on a blog https://extraordinarydrawers.wordpress.com/ The photos we received were indeed extraordinary! A drawer containing a rabbi's treasures alongside some precious possessions of his Japanese wife. A Sikh woman's turban drawer. A drawer full of baby clothes including a cannula through which the mother received a bone marrow transfusion that saved her life, and many more. Through this very simple challenge we could see the rich diversity and nuance of human story, borne out by everyday artefacts hidden away in private homes. We could hear people's stories explored and shared in touching ways and with new insight into the richness of their lives. So often our testimonies are also our eulogies, but through creative spaces we can open up the rich variety of human story in new ways and bear witness to our faith to others.

Through creativity we engage with processes that go beyond our intentions, they acquire a sort of transcendence and cause us to ask, 'What is the source?' And surely, this is our prime calling as the Church, to be fearless in exploring the edges of existence, to look for that which supersedes us, within the everyday experiences of life.

Stories are written and told in words and narrative, but also in the language of colour, light, abstraction. Through creativity we are given a door to a new depth of story, a way of telling that can be multi-dimensional and questioning, teasing us and dementing us. For me, this is the door to seeing the world with fresh eyes and sometimes to glimpse the Creator who imagined us in the first place.

POINT OF CONNECTION

How could we encourage creative diversity in our Christian communities? How could church be less word-centred and free to explore the rich variety of creativity that surrounds us? What one practical thing could we do to enable our Church to be more colourful?

POINT OF REFLECTION

In the 1960s two Methodist people collected works of art in order to open up faith conversations, this collection was subsequently given to the British Methodist Church as an art collection. Many of the works reflect the life and teaching of Jesus and include artists such as Graham Sutherland, Elizabeth Frink, William Roberts and Patrick Heron. To find out more about the Methodist Modern Art Collection you can visit the Methodist Church Website. Why not make the collection the subject of some group conversations in your place?

PRAYER

Imagined out of nothing
drawn onto the blank canvas of the
universe
spoken in story and laughter
struggle and colour
Creative God may we play in the infinite
hues of your love,
exploring the edges and spaces of time
and feasting on the glorious dance of life

Chapter 9
GROWING STORIES: RESPONDING TO CONTEXT

Here, Barbara explores some stories of mission and offers a personal narrative and some theological reflection in a weaving of contexts, experience and faith.

In 1887, Samuel Pollard, a Cornish Bible Christian gave up his proposed career in the civil service and boarded a square-rigged sailing vessel heading for China. He was 22 years old. Changing ship in Colombo he arrived in Shanghai three months later. He then travelled a further 1500 miles up the Yangstse River to arrive at the mission station in Zaotong, a house so small that his horse was stabled in the kitchen.

Later, Eama Hainge, a missionary nurse from Birmingham joined him. Together they founded a school and a missionary college in the mountain region of Shimenkhan and raised their family. Samuel grew a pigtail and learned the local languages and then, working from first principles, he set about developing a script to translate the Bible into the language of the local Miao people.

In 1915 he died and was buried in the mountains of Shimenkhan. Eama returned to England with their sons. In 1950 all remaining English missionaries were ordered to leave and the country remained closed to foreigners until 1995. The Miao people buried their Bible, prayed in secret and learned how to survive through China's Cultural Revolution.

This story is both extraordinary and commonplace, especially in Methodist heritage. There was an era when people were inspired to spread the gospel to the ends of the earth, setting off at a moment's notice and at great personal peril. Fifty years after Samuel's death, a child growing up in a small Kentish town had the first stirrings of vocation as she listened to returning Methodist missionaries telling of their adventures across the globe. It resulted in lots of JMA ribbons, singing of rallying hymns ... 'This is our story, this is our song!' and a first awareness of a bigger world 'out there'. I was clear that I was called into ministry when I was 16, but at that point women couldn't be ordained, so unlike Samuel Pollard, I went and did something else.

What is the nature of Samuel's story, is it one of triumph or well-meaning foolishness? Or worse, is it such a damaging part of our colonial history that it is better repented? Certainly there is plenty of evidence that we often confuse faith sharing with expansionism and imposing our culture without proper regard for context. If we think this only true of the past then it is salutary to read a recent story of the murder of a 26-year-old American missionary John Allen Chau, allegedly killed by islanders of North Sentinel, a forbidden island in the Andaman Sea.[1] Indian law says that the island is a protected territory and its inhabitants should be left completely alone; it is currently too dangerous to retrieve Mr Chau's body. He had wanted to spread the gospel there.

I want to follow this story in several directions, like tributaries of a river. The tributaries diverge, meander and re-join in a very different landscape. I do so, not to answer the above questions, but to return to them differently. I will begin in a completely different continent.

Hermannsburg is an Aboriginal community in Ljirapinta Ward of the MacDonnell Shire in the Northern Territory of Australia, 125km south west of Alice Springs. It was named such by two Lutheran missionaries, after their home town in Germany. It is a sacred site of the Aranda people, associated with the Aranda Ratapa Dreaming. (Dreamtime is the foundation of Aboriginal religion and culture. It dates back some 65,000 years. It is the story of events that have happened, how the universe came to be, how human beings were created and how their Creator intended for humans to function within the world as they knew it. Aboriginal people understood the Dreamtime as a beginning that never ended. They held the belief that the Dreamtime is a period on a continuum of past, present and future.)

Like Samuel Pollard, the Hermannsburg missionaries learned the local language and engaged with local people, developing a dictionary of the Aranda language and providing facilities for the community as well as baptising local children and providing church services. There were various times of hostility between the missionaries and the traditional owners, but mission work continued until 1982 when the land was handed back under the Aboriginal Land Rights Act. It is now protected by the National Trust of Australia as a heritage site.

Throughout the last two centuries Aboriginal culture has been barbarically violated in certain parts of Australia. Many people were shot, abused or considered little more than animals. And yet, Aboriginal culture has survived in many areas, through story-telling and song. For Aboriginal people, the link between story and land is crucial, stories have a geographical place to be told. There is much more to be said here, but this tributary takes an interesting twist.

Alice Springs is the 'Red Centre' of Australia and as such has its own particular culture. The soil is dry and the rains come infrequently. There is a powerful presence of the earth, the landscape and the vegetation that hunkers down for many years waiting for rain. The Ghost Gums cling to the sides of the road or mark the path of the dry riverbed. The scale of this landscape diminishes human importance. You either love Alice or loathe it; people try to leave and are drawn back to it; it is a place where land has a voice. There are many rich seams of culture, painting that reflects Aboriginal story, horticulture that must honour the arid environment and music. In particular there is the Central Australian Women's Choir.

The 32 members of the Central Australian Women's Choir have a fascinating repertoire. Alongside their traditional obligations, they have kept alive their rich heritage of song and story, singing songs in the traditional languages of Pitjantjatjara and West Arrande but also in English and German. The choir recently made a trip to Germany where they performed their songs, but also re-taught the Lutheran Church some of the traditional hymns and tunes that they had preserved from the times in Hermannsburg of the missionaries, songs that the German church had long forgotten. This story is documented in the film, *The Song Keepers.*

Here we see a complex and intricate mixing of cultures and story, European missionaries, colonial expansion, Aboriginal dreaming, misunderstanding, antagonism and separation. But also a redemption as this gracious, joyful, forgiving group of women 'return the song' to a distant land whilst they also re-find and cherish the songlines of their own landscapes.

POINT OF CONNECTION

These two stories are both similar and very different because of their different cultural context. Can we think of stories that only make sense in our culture? Where do we find culture and story mixing in our own neighbourhoods?

POINT OF REFLECTION

Jesus told stories at a particular time and culture. Can we transfer them to our own culture and how does mission look different with hindsight?

A personal narrative and a return

Now to follow another tributary.

Following my call to be a missionary, I was commissioned by the World Church Department of the Methodist Church in Britain to serve overseas in Zambia. As it happened I never made it, my life took a number of other twists and turns and I was eventually ordained to the Methodist Ministry when I was 40. However, I vaguely remember being commissioned to be a missionary, at a formal and solemn ceremony somewhere in the North of England, it was a serious commitment even though the river was not flowing in the direction I had anticipated. Life continued, ministry in Liverpool and then in Bradford. As a Southerner, learning to live in the strange lands of the North, experiencing what it means to live in Pakistani-heritage Britain, in places where accents, traditions and rituals are alien from my own. The stories of the Scriptures have continually been my anchor, challenge and reference points, 'Love your enemy and pray for those who persecute you', 'Hold fast to that which is good', 'How do we sing the Lord's song in a strange land?', 'Nothing can separate us from the love of God in Christ Jesus'. And the stories of Jesus, the persistence of the father waiting for his son, the perplexity of a woman sitting at a well, the breaking in of transformative love in walking and sharing bread...these and many more Biblical narratives have been the sustenance for the journey, the signposts in a changing world.

These stories have been broken open over and over, as we made bread together in Liverpool. As I walked the streets of Bradford hearing no English spoken. As my sons were held at knife point in a household break-in. In all the questions and perplexity of being Christian in a Britain that no longer finds its home within the Christian faith. These narratives have remained a constant reminder of being part of a much bigger story, one that is not yet complete, and will only make sense when all things are called back into God's timeless love.

It is only recently that I discovered that my commissioning to be a missionary all those years ago, a calling I thought I had failed to fulfil, was actually in the Eastbrook Hall in Bradford – the church that closed in order for Touchstone to be formed, the place in which I have located the last ten years of my ministry. The place where I discovered what mission is about.

So, the tributaries of the river meander through our lives, but the river remains the same, the living water, promised us by Jesus. The story of another way to understand the course of things, a way to resist the dominant narratives of consumerism, capitalism and environmental destruction. A perpetual call towards the ocean of God's redeeming love for ourselves and the whole of creation. We will find no rest until we find our rest here.

Finally, let's follow another tributary.

In 2017 a group of people visited China as part of a Churches Together in Britain and Ireland delegation to forge links with the church that is currently the fastest growing in the world. It was wonderful to be invited to be part of this journey. It is impossible to gain accurate statistics as the church is both official and unofficial in Chinese culture, but an estimate is that there will be approximately 247 million Chinese Christians by 2030, a number exceeding the predicted number of Christians in the USA. Whatever the accurate statistics and reasons are, there is certainly a phenomenal rise in adherence to faith in China that the CTBI group wanted to see. Unlike Samuel Pollard, this group travelled by plane, train and minibus and arrived in Shanghai within three days. They were greeted by English speaking leaders, by skyscrapers and neon signs advertising Armani. It is not only Christianity that is growing in China, but also the economy, the migration to the urban environment and such global initiatives at the Belt and Road. (The Belt and Road initiative is a development strategy of the Chinese government, involving massive infrastructure development across Europe, Asia and Africa. The 'Belt' refers to overland routes whilst the 'road' refers to sea routes) The small group of representatives from England, Ireland and Scotland arrived in Shimenkhan with their translators, guides, umbrellas and luggage on a rainy day in August. The hills were green and the roads were tarmac and they ate a welcome meal of noodles in a local hotel. As far as I am aware, there were no horses in the kitchen.

After lunch, we made our way towards the Church, from which there was a clearly audible sound of singing. This small building was packed with people in traditional costume, bright with embroidery, hair plaited, babies in their arms. These were the Miao people, singing a welcome. The song was 'Blessed Assurance, Jesus is mine …' the hymn that they had learned from Samuel Pollard, before he died, before Eama left, before they had buried their Bibles, before the graves had been desecrated, before the Cultural revolution, before the foreigners had to leave, before they had to pray in secret, before they had been persecuted for being Christian, before the road had come, before WiFi, TV and Levi jeans, 'this is our story, this is our song …'. The song I had sung when I still believed in missionaries and bravado and the English right to take our version of the gospel to the heathen world. And the visitors remembered it too, and everyone cried when the old, old lady with no teeth hugged us tightly and said, 'Thank you for coming back!'

And that, in a way would be a great end to the story, because we want to hear the news that the Christian Amity Foundation in China has not only published more than 180 million Bibles, which are exported all over the world, but also that we can lay flowers on the grave of Samuel Pollard and feel that we are not so guilty of colonial violations that exterminated communities. We want to know that somehow there is redemption and salvation in this temporal story, that life and love is triumphing over death and destruction and we are redeemed by history. But the story isn't finished yet, the water still flows along the tributaries.

POINT OF CONNECTION

Sometimes, events in our lives only make sense later. Can you think of examples where something that happened to you suddenly found a place in your story?

POINT OF REFLECTION

Not only does our colonial history look different with time, both more awful and more nuanced, but we haven't really faced it yet or worked out our identities in relation to historical decisions made by an Empire or on the whim of religious fervour. We remain in the turmoil of our own history and in the environment of post-colonialism that we have invited to places like Bradford. We are not only facing our lack of Empire but a sharp critique of our colonial past. The oblique light thrown on our history casts long shadows too. Shadows we walk through every day as we find what it means to be multicultural Britain.

Yet, we still want to love our enemies, to hold fast to that which is good, to remember the songs of our forebears and sing them afresh in this strange land. I wonder how these stories, both personal and collective, can continue to bridge the gap between life and faith?

Songlines

In the summer of 2018 I visited Alice Springs to stay with some friends who live there. It was my first visit to Australia and so an impressive experience. There is a certain timelessness about the Aboriginal way of life, after all, if you have been the traditional owners of a land for in excess of 60,000 years then it's understandable you are going to take the long view. The last time Aboriginal people first encountered Western culture was in 1984 – 'we weren't a lost tribe' they insisted, 'just separated from our relatives, and other members of the Pintupi clan'. The Aboriginal Dreaming is at the heart of Aboriginal self-understanding. The Dreaming is a gift of ancient stories revealed at certain parts of the vast landscapes that give both identity and meaning. The secrets of the Dreaming are passed from generation to generation by the ancestors and give the 'songlines' by which the journeys of these nomadic people are remembered. The Earth and the people are part of the same narratives, the stories can only be told 'on country'.

Dreaming is not part of Western culture but maybe we also have songlines? Maybe Methodists, who are known for 'singing the faith', understand this in a particular way. As the memories of our recent lives, the stories of our forebears and the stories of the earth intertwine to form the complex narratives of life. Some stories buried and unearthed later, others held in the songs hummed in kitchens or sung in worship, through which our theology is worked and reworked from one generation to the next. Like the Miao people of China and the residents of Hermannsburg, the songs that we remember bring to mind the heart of who we are and articulate the essence of our faith in ways that other words don't match. We are continually called to sing the Lord's song as strangers, and whilst doing so recognise the eternal connection between our personal stories, our sacred texts and our theological understanding. Stories and songs not only result in theology, they are theology, the medium by which the mystery of our creation and identity are held within the narratives of faith; as such they are a rich source of revelation and transforming hope.

When my mother was very old, she didn't necessarily know who we were, but if we sang to her then she would connect with us in a new way. She knew the words of songs and prayers even when she couldn't remember faces or names. These song memories are held very close to our hearts, found in a different part of our brains, connected with our life narrative in unique ways. The hymn 'Blessed Assurance Jesus is Mine' feels pretty dated these days yet despite the fact that I now struggle with much of the theology it expresses it can still evoke a powerful sense of belonging and connection with my own story and others across the world. We know that this sense of sung narrative connects us with certain times and places in our everyday life – I can't for instance hear The Beatles' song 'Hey Jude' without being immediately transported back to the school bus! I wonder how we can remember the Lord's song in this strange land and find the songlines that connect life, faith and culture in new ways? Rather than 'singing religious songs', how can we evoke a sense of God's presence through the poetry and challenge of song and in doing so resist the closed-down narratives of our colonial past? How can we sing the songs of liberation and justice that could transform the world and how can we express the infinite love of the Creator without having to repeat verses of nonsense? What is the music of our souls, where are our songlines?

With all these questions in mind return to Samuel and Eama Pollard who set off from Cornwall so many years ago on a venture that was both wonderful and foolish, and to the thought that only God knows the end of these stories that take so many twists and turns, touch so many lives and sometimes disappear from view only to surface later and be interpreted differently. To trust our stories to God is to know that with hindsight we might make different choices but also to know that there is forgiveness in the mistakes if we endeavour to hold fast to the good. So let's live our own stories with courage and hope, knowing they will only be understood in God's timeless perspective.

As I have tried to show in this roller coaster of a chapter, stories are not linear or one dimensional, they weave and twist backwards and forwards, picking us up and putting us in a different place. We can admire other people's stories from afar, only to find that they involve us more intimately than we imagined, our story is not isolated from the context and communities around us. Stories live as we do!

POINT OF CONNECTION
Which songs or hymns take you back to a certain time or place? Are there hymns that you once loved but now you cannot agree with the theology or sentiment?

POINT OF REFLECTION
I wonder whether you have read a novel or seen a film that reflects on our colonial history and how we might understand a story differently because of those insights.

PRAYER

Nomadic God, sing your song in us
Put the tune of your gospel in our adventures,
In our hearts, in our wandering
Redeem our foolish good intentions
Remind us that we are not strangers to you
Call us home to you, singing.

Chapter 10

SHOCKING STORIES: HANDLING BAD STUFF

This chapter faces head on the fact that Christians have not always been a good advert for God. It acknowledges too that the Bible contains some difficult material. Clive considers how Christians are to handle stories and traditions about past practices, ideas and beliefs which remain in the Christian memory.

As indicated in Chapter 2, my own story was interwoven from the start with troubling stories. By that I mean that though I was immersed in, learned from, and began to inhabit the Christian story in a positive way, I was also being soaked by other stories too: stories which suggested that perhaps Roman Catholics weren't real Christians, that black people were obviously intellectually inferior to whites, that people from Kirkby could be trusted less than people from St. Helens, that the North Wales coast was a lot nicer than the Costa del Sol. I couldn't control all of these, and seemingly trivial narratives mingled with stories that could kindle deep prejudice. As we go through life, a major task presents itself: to sift and test the stories within which we live and to work out which ones we affirm, which we oppose, and which we want to tell differently. Some such stories can raise a smile, because we can identify them as local prejudice, change our attitudes and behaviour and move on. Some are dangerous and damaging. Alongside the task of listening to painful stories, of encouraging people to have the courage to voice accounts of abuse, or of marginalization, there is also the task of identifying, confronting and taking account of stories within the Christian tradition itself, and within our own life experiences, that are not positive or helpful stories. Yet they are there; they have influenced us; if they are in the Bible they remain there, as part of scripture. If they're part of Christian history – even from a distant place – they're embarrassing. If they're stories of local church life, they stick and fester, whether we like it or not. What do we do with them?

The Jephthah effect

I must have been in my late twenties before I even realized that the story of Jephthah's daughter existed, let alone was in the Bible (Judges 11:29-40). To cut a long-ish story short: Jephthah promises to make a sacrifice of whoever he happens to see first, if he successfully leads the Israelites in the conquering of the Ammonites. His success means he must see his daughter sacrificed for his victory in order to keep his vow. The story stands as a warning to the practice of vow-making, is a witness to the low status accorded to women throughout most of human history and the shocking effects of male domination and violence.

The summary I have just made is itself, though, rather defensive. It tries to suggest a value for the story. It tries to offer a kind of rationale for why the story remains there and is useful. In truth, it is the only realistic way of making a claim for why we might still read the story. The integrity of the biblical canon may demand that we do this in some way. If we are to hold on to a notion that an authoritative collection of texts is useful for a religious community to carry with it, then it is not wise to jettison the bits we might not like later on. We might then want to jettison different bits at different times but later want to reinstate some texts thrown out earlier. In the case of the Christian Bible, we do best to acknowledge that it is a collection of texts which we receive, warts and all, and have to wrestle with even if it contains some shocking stories or views. God is, after all, with us by God's Spirit as we receive these texts and as we continue to work with them as a living community.

So how is the story of Jephthah's daughter a 'bad story'? It's a bad story not because it is badly told. It is a troubling story that confronts us with shocking truths about how human beings can act, and men especially. We're suggesting that it is a 'bad story' if we try to pretend that such behaviour is acceptable.

The Jephthah Effect, then, is the recognition that all human communities, and all human individuals, carry with them tales of what is *not* acceptable, as well as stories which are meant to build up and encourage. What is not acceptable, though, is not always as immediately apparent as it is here. The theme of the oppression of women runs through the whole Christian Bible, even if there are also stories of strong, defiant women, and material suggesting that the demeaning of women must be challenged (Deborah, Ruth, Orpah, Esther, Mary Magdalene, Lydia, Priscilla, Galatians 3:25-29). The fact of slavery is there too, mixing the message and experience of the release from bondage (Exodus) with recognition that slavery persisted and was not always opposed by Christians (Philemon). Simply because stories are *there* in the Bible does not, then, mean that what is portrayed is acceptable. The living communities that make up the Church exist to enable Bible-readers/hearers to interpret and use the Bible wisely and to handle critically whatever material needs a re-think.

Bad Stories from Christian history

'We all make mistakes.' Such a statement, easily made, can be used to justify all manner of evil deeds. It is wholly consistent with the Apostle Paul's summary of what we are all like ('all have sinned and fall short of the glory of God', Rom. 3.23). It can also apply to a great many accounts of Christian behavior throughout Christian history across the last two millennia. 'We all make mistakes' can, though, become a glib remark. It becomes the broom with which past actions, sometimes horrendous, can be brushed under the carpet of history in the hope that they are forgotten about. Rather than being woven into the fabric of Christianity's complex story they are simply suppressed.

In the same way, however, as the Bible contains 'bad stories' – uncomfortable tales of awful things from the past – so also Christian history includes multiple examples of actions which, with hindsight, are simply difficult to believe were undertaken in God's name. However generous we might wish to be in reviewing the past ('they could not have known better', 'they acted in good faith', 'their intentions were just and true'), some past actions are simply indefensible. Here are a few examples.

Iconoclasm

Christians smashed up beautiful artwork at various times in Christian history, believing that because God could and should not be portrayed in any form of human image (for a graven image would become an idol) therefore statues and pictures had to be opposed. Sometimes, statues were hidden away and brought out again later. Murals were painted over. Large statues could be more easily destroyed than shifted. These stories of destructive Christian behaviour are part of Christian history and need to be kept there as a reminder of just how nasty Christians can be to each other. They can also steer appropriately the way in which we respond to contemporary news stories. The Taliban's destruction of large, ancient statues of the Buddha in Afghanistan in 2001 was not something which only 'others' do. It was vandalism, undertaken for religious reasons, and was as unacceptable as any Christian activity to destroy the religious imagery of another group.

Crusading

One definition of 'to crusade' is to 'make an effort to achieve something that you believe in strongly'. This is an understatement when some of the stories of the late medieval period's Christian crusades against Islam are heard. It is not known precisely how many thousands of Jews and Muslims may have been slaughtered at the hands of Christian crusaders in the siege, and then massacre, of Jerusalem in 1099. But although the conventions of battle may have been different from today, slaughter remains slaughter. If undertaken in the name of religion it is especially and poignantly tragic as it evidences human attempts to act directly on behalf of God, as if we have perceived once and for all what God wills. Human history contains, however, so many examples of failed human attempts to discern and enact the will of God that caution in understanding how God's Kingdom is to be welcomed into the world is clearly needed. The stories of the crusades are needed as part of Christian history both as a witness to what people thought they were meant to do 'in good faith', yet also as a record of how distorted and twisted all our wills and desires can become.

Politicking with princes

The great German Reformer, Martin Luther (1483-1546) is a personal hero of mine. The intensity of his faith, his wit and powerful rhetoric, and his overwhelming insistence on God's prior action and the fruitlessness of human agency with respect to salvation have all been profoundly influential on generations of Christians. To tell Luther's story, though, as if he were a modern Christian, with a relaxed approach to life, a calm demeanour, who avoided conflict if he could, had all his theology neatly worked out and was even-handed in his dealings with all would be to misrepresent him. He had a foul mouth at times, uttered some shocking things about Jews, was deliberately provocative in his relations with (Catholic) Christians of his time and often came across as arrogant. He also made some tough political calls which had huge – at times fatal – consequences for his contemporaries. There are many reasons why it is understandable he did not support the overworked and under-rewarded peasants who protested against increasing princely control and higher taxation. By not supporting the peasants, however, and actively encouraging the political leaders (princes) to crush the peasant revolts, Luther was choosing the wealthy over the poor. His rhetoric and political choices led to tens of thousands of deaths in the 1524-5 Peasants' War. Any account of Luther's life cannot leave this, and other negative aspects of his character and views, out of his story.

Colonial expansionism

'Was the British Empire a good thing, or not?' sounds like a school or college essay title ('Discuss'). Simple answers may well be offered (yes or no!), though the story and stories of Empire are indeed many and complex. Whole studies exist of how missionary activity linked with colonial expansion. There is no escaping the fact that at times Christianity paved the way for military and economic expansion and missionary Christians simply assumed and asserted that Christianity is the best religion (and should replace whatever was found locally – be it in Africa, Asia, Oceania or the Americas). Whatever good influence it might also have been able to have, Christianity could at times promote White supremacy and work hand-in-glove with ruthless capitalism and military domination.

Those four stories from Christian history are merely easy-to-grasp examples of difficult aspects of Christianity's past. They need to be there so that we remember that the conduct of the church, and of individual Christians, is fraught with ambiguity, riddled with evidence of poor choices and had awful consequences at times. Even if Christians in the past believed – just as we do now – they were trying to make good ethical choices, they often failed miserably. We have to remember how wrong things sometimes went.

POINT OF REFLECTION
What particular examples from Christianity's past have come to mind as you've been reading this chapter? What makes you ashamed when you look back at Christianity's history?

Closer to home?

But that was all in the distant past! What's it got to do with us? Even if we accept that we have to confront our own 'bad stories', surely they're easier to handle. We know what happened, we know what we did wrong, and we've been forgiven (even if we don't forget) for what we did as we move on. Well, maybe. It is likely, though, that some of our own 'bad stories' – things we might not tell very often, or only to those who know us well; things we're not proud of, which have not been true to who we believe ourselves to be and the faith we profess – are the 'Big' Christian stories taking shape at local level. Racism, for example, is insidious, is embedded across Western cultures and creates huge problems in society. This includes churches, especially when white Christians (and we speak as two white Christians) do not recognize their own privilege and are impervious to the many implicit ways in which black and Asian World Majority groups are frequently excluded. This is especially the case with exclusion from decision-making positions in church life. Such patterns of Christian behaviour and ecclesial life are but continuing local forms of colonial and imperialist activity.

Denominational histories also run deep and continue to have lasting and local effects. A good example of this is the material brought together in the 'Church, State and Establishment' report which was brought to the British Methodist Conference of 2004. Though a dry church report in many ways, it was striking that the report began (in paragraphs 11 to 22) with a series of stories about what ecumenical relations *actually felt like*. Rather than disappear quickly into 'committee-speak' the working party wanted the real experience of actual inter-church encounter to be reflected in concrete examples. As the report itself acknowledged:

> Aspects of identity, instinctive attitudes, differences and conflict are often named through the telling of stories and experiences. Yet it must also be acknowledged that

people often recall their bad experiences more quickly than the good, even when the bad experiences were the exception. The most easily remembered stories are not always complimentary and certainly not unbiased. (Paragraph 23)[1]

It is often not easy to distinguish between event, memory, story, anecdote and evidence. For researchers and scholars, anecdotes cannot be enough when dealing with historical events and human relations. Stories can sometimes, though, capture truth even when they are not verifiable, and not able to count as evidence. Bad stories can thus be accounts of bad things that mix potentially verifiable material with impressions, opinions and feelings. It may well be the impressions, opinions and feelings that most need dealing with.

The negative may surface more easily than the positive but this chapter wants us to face the negative stuff. If we don't, then we can't deal with it, or let God help us deal with it. We have to report the bad stuff from past and present and acknowledge openly and honestly when we're responsible directly for the bad stuff, or implicated within it, even when it seems historical, or happening elsewhere. The global *is* the local. The past *is* within the present. Both of these observations have to be respected.

Some practical strategies

So how do we handle, individually and communally, the bad stories we encounter? A simple response is to remind ourselves that we need 'reading strategies'. That's a posh way of saying we need to find ways of knowing how we are processing whatever stories we hear or read. Everyone reads from a particular set of *perspectives*. Initially we might not even know what they are. It's useful to ask ourselves hard questions so we find out. (Be it as an Asian person, a white person, as a man, an Irish person, a straight person, a middle-class citizen, a gay person: how am I hearing this story?) We can then acknowledge those perspectives as we read, so they don't distort our reading via their hiddenness, but become part of our way of reading.

As well as those aspects of who we are, though, we might then *choose* particular perspectives to read from. These become reading strategies. As a white person I cannot choose to be anything other than white, but I can listen to the ways in which other readers, from different ethnic backgrounds, read or hear the same story. There is currently much discussion across the world in all forms of education about the need for post-colonial reading strategies. This is simply because so much has happened from a colonial perspective: choices about what should be read and studied, how it should be read and by whom. It is high time that *what* is commended to be heard and read by all, and *how* we all read and hear, is re-thought. The Bible is always likely to survive any critical review, though not all would agree for precisely the kind of reasons we have looked at in this chapter. *How* the Bible is read needs very careful thought.

Perspectives are like spectacles. Sometimes we're wearing them without realizing – lots of different pairs of them, in fact. When they become reading strategies, they are pairs of spectacles we are choosing to wear, because they give us an important insight into what a text or story might actually be most 'about', or how it might be best understood.

'Bad stories', then, are simply part of human history, and always will be. To try to write better stories includes carrying and handling the bad stories that will remain with us.

PRAYER

Forgiving God,
you know our failings and faults,
yet you stick with us.
You know the pasts we have inherited
and the pasts we have made for ourselves.
Release us from the burdens of the past;
remind us of the wrongs committed;
while accompanying us into new life:
as we remember what needs to be
remembered,
but are freed to live according to your will and
purpose.
In the name of Jesus the Liberator we pray

Amen.

Chapter 11

INHABITING STORIES: LIVING IT OUT

This chapter takes the first of two steps to round off the book. In each of these final two chapters we ask what all of our listening and story-telling mean in practice. First, Clive explores the ways in which Christian faith is like and unlike performing a script.

So what? After ten chapters of exploring what stories are, how stories work, the contexts they come from and relate to, our own stories, the Christian story, unheard stories, other faith stories, Gospel stories and uncomfortable stories, where are we? We've already anticipated some of what we need to do with all of this. We need *to listen* a lot for one thing. There are stories that still need to be uncovered that have an impact on the content of our faith. We also need to do a fair amount of *digging and resource-gathering*. This is an ongoing task. Exploration of the Bible, of Christian history, and of contemporary world Christianity can be both fun and informative. It gives us more to draw on as we live Christian lives. When we access the Christian story, and seek to live our lives within it, we have to be helped to discern how our believing, belonging, behaving and thinking can all be shaped constructively by the stories which make up that 'big story.' But what does this mean in practice? In this and the next chapter we look more closely at what is entailed in concrete, practical terms. What does 'living the Gospel' through living (within) the Story/stories which God supplies, and which the Christian tradition carries with it, actually entail?

Following a script?

It may be thought by now that the Christian story provides a script. All we need to do, then, is learn the script ('do this, do that') and all manner of things will be well. Certain words and convictions, particular actions, specific beliefs can all be adopted and practiced and then the task of 'living the Gospel' can be achieved by 'inhabiting the script'. As Christians, we are, it may be assumed, actors who live according to God's script. Our job is to slot into what God has laid out, learn the lines, and perform the play.

There is, of course, some truth in this. The tradition gives us images, concepts, ideas, metaphors with which to work. The 'Kingdom of God' gives us an overarching concept for grasping how and where God reigns. We (try to) live within it now, whilst acknowledging it is yet to come fully. 'Church' is also a concrete reality and an ideal concept at one and the same time. We are very familiar with its fallible local forms whilst also knowing what the local communities to which we belong are aiming for, and we even get glimpses of what the church, at its best, can be at times. We recognize a tension between 'script' and 'practice'. We also live out a script when we participate in Christian ritual and engage in Christian practices. Baptism, Holy Communion, worship generally, pastoral visiting, pilgrimage, voluntary work of all kinds, are ways of living out Christian faith.

We gain much more than a glimpse of God and God's activity by looking at Jesus. But when we seek to live 'in Christ' and follow Jesus we do more than simply live according to a prescribed script. Even if we don't sit down at every turn and theorize about it, following Jesus becomes shorthand for quite a complex reflection process as we live the Christian life. We don't just copy Jesus ethically, though we do follow his example. We don't just look back to a past figure (Jesus of Nazareth); we accept God is present now 'in Christ'. We don't just refer to Jesus in the present as a spiritual presence, for the embodiment of the incarnate God will not allow us. There is more to the (concrete, fleshy, embodied) God than *just* the Spirit of Christ. Talk of 'performing a script' does not, then, do justice to the configuration of activities and reflective processes at work here.

Living the Story/stories, living the Gospel, being a Christian, then, are in some ways like performing a script, but unlike such a practice in so many ways that we need to push further to become more clear about what is going on.

POINT OF REFLECTION

Think of some examples of when living the Christian life *does* feel like performing a script? What is helpful and unhelpful in the examples you have brought to mind?

Think of some examples of when living the Christian life *clearly doesn't* feel like performing a script? What is helpful and unhelpful in the examples you have brought to mind?

Involvement in the story of God: some practicalities

If we ask ourselves 'What's the point of being Christian?' then there's a simple answer: it is to enjoy life to the full. This is not to be understood in a selfish, individualistic way as if we're on some kind of isolated self-help journey of self-discovery. For we can only flourish if all have the opportunity to flourish (and that means the whole living world). Enjoying life to the full can only come about in our own lives, we believe, by living life within, and in relation to, God. As Christians we believe that we have seen sufficient of what God is like because of Jesus Christ. Yet if the Christian life isn't in any simple sense performing the script, but the stories we have talked about are important, then how do we access and make use of the ones which are given to us (in Bible and Tradition)? And how do we use the ones we hear and tell in our own lives? Let's do some recapping.

A way of reading the previous chapters is as follows:

- It is important to tell our own life stories, and to tell them (to ourselves and to each other) honestly and creatively (Chapters 2 and 8). In this way we can see what has been helping us grow, what's been limiting or damaging, and what influences upon us have made us who we are (Chapters 2 and 10). God's activity will always have been interweaving with our own story. Where we are able to highlight that and enable our own story to be explicitly part of God's story too (as testimony) then it would be good for us and for others if we do that (Chapter 4).

- For us to tell our story as testimony, we need to know something of God, as the church bears witness to God as known in Christ, by the Spirit. We can access all sorts of resources which the Christian tradition has assembled through time to enable us to do that (Chapters 3 and 6).

- The story of God is being told beyond us, as Christians, as well as amongst us. God is at work at and beyond the margins of the church, and within the lives of people in the church who may not have found it easy to tell their stories (Chapter 5). God's story is also told beyond the church in, and between, other religious traditions (Chapter 7). There are also tricky and uncomfortable aspects of the way that the Christian story has been, and is being, told which need to be taken account of (Chapters 9 and 10).

So what do we do next? The exhilarating thing about thinking of our Christian lives as testimonies is the humbling sense that we can be part of God's story *at all*. We are not the creators of the story which God is enabling to unfold in human history – the story of peace and reconciliation in the face of hostility, of the quest for justice, and for individual and communal well-being. We participate in it. Yet God invites us to take up the melody and improvise with it. Improvisation is a powerful image which many Christian theologians have taken up in recent years. Improvisation is an aspect of performance in a number of musical forms, though is especially associated with jazz. Within the framework of a piece of jazz music, different instrumentalists (pianists, drummers, saxophonists, trumpeters, for example) are invited to offer a solo around the basic theme, riffing on the melody introduced. Though hearers not used to such solos may be inclined to say, 'It sounds like she's just making it up as she goes along', that's because she is! It is important to recognize, though, that improvisation is only possible when a is: a) a very accomplished instrumentalist, b) feels comfortable enough with, and trusting enough of, the players with whom she plays, and c) knows enough about the style and genre of the music within which the melody is offered.

Improvising the Gospel is no different from this. Because living a life of faith is not simply performing a script, God invites us to follow the melody presented to us, inspired by the Spirit, seeking Christ in all things, people and places, and welcoming the Kingdom where its inbreaking is evident. We become better improvisers as we keep on practising, seeking to be ever more proficient in our skills of discernment, recognizing the melody God has given us. We do this by enhancing our skills as instrumentalists. Anyone who has ever tried to learn a musical instrument, or had to listen to someone else in the house learning a musical instrument, knows how taxing this can be. Repeated drum-thumping, a squawking violin, a whining electric guitar: all of these can seem a long way from a concert performance or gig. Yet all musicians not only have to start somewhere; they have to keep on working at it. This is the same with the genuinely enjoyable practice of working at, and with, the Christian story. But what does it mean to practice one's skill and art, like a jazz improviser, in order to be a more proficient participant in God's story?

Topping up and drawing from the reservoir

You'll remember that in speaking of how life stories become testimonies we were reminded that we need to make links between things that happen to us and stories, insights, themes and characters from the Christian tradition. Then we will be able to explore and test how we are to understand our experience in relation to God. We do not do this on our own. Nor is it always an easy process. It is, though, important to recognize that we need to *know* something about the Bible's contents, and something about Christian tradition and history to enable us to make these connections. 'We', here, means the church. We can do much ourselves, but we discuss with others as we make links in order to be able to offer our testimonies.

It's useful to think of the wide range of materials on which we might draw as a reservoir. Each time we work with others to help us understand our experience in relation to God, we dip into the reservoir and drink from it. The reservoir of resources can, though, run dry. We can use things up. We need to ensure that the water supply is topped up, in the sense that we need to keep refreshing our familiarity with the rich tradition on which we draw. It isn't, of course, true that the Bible runs dry, or the tradition fades; but they will dry up *for us* if we do not keep on interacting with them or keep adding to our own (individual and collective) awareness of what's in them. Topping up the reservoir is, then, just another way of saying that in order to keep on participating in the Christian story (living the Christian life) and to keep on being able to interpret and present life events as testimony, we need to keep our engagement with the resources available to us as fresh as possible.

Having more and more knowledge of the Bible and tradition doesn't make you a better Christian, of course. What it does mean is that you have more to draw on when needed. The deeper the reservoir, and the more you keep it topped up, the more you have to choose from and the more it may enrich you. With respect to the Bible, then, the more you know is in there, the more materials you have to link up with and make use of in interpreting your experience. Likewise, the more aspects of the Christian tradition you're familiar with, the more you can connect with in creative ways. It's not the fact of knowing that matters, it's what you do with what you know. And because two heads are better than one, and ten heads better still, the process of drawing from the reservoir of Bible, tradition, and history as a group means that more resources will be drawn on and used.

Ultimately this is about enrichment, though not in a selfish way. It is about recognizing how all can tap into the full life that God makes available. This is what inhabiting the Story means. It's active, life-enhancing participation in God's living story. We learn more about our faith's tradition not for the sake of it, or to win points in a general knowledge quiz. We do it because it enables not just our personal development, but the fulfilment of God's story intended for all.

POINT OF REFLECTION

Thinking of the Bible, with which books, or sections of the Bible, are you most familiar, and make most use of? Which books or sections of the Bible do you barely look at? Any idea why?

The faith communities we form (including even churches at times!), in and through which we inhabit the tradition, are also the contexts in which we top up the reservoir. They do enrich; they do enhance … at their best. We need, though, to issue a word of caution. In a challenging article, Valentin Dedji, drawing on his capacity to look at the UK from both Western African and British perspectives, makes this statement:

> The scandal of the Church is that the Christ-event is no longer life-changing; it has become life-enhancing. We have lost the power and joy that makes real disciples; we have become consumers of religion and not disciples of Jesus Christ.[1]

This is a telling judgment on the rather insipid forms of Christianity which are often evident in the UK today. It's clear what is being said here: life-enhancing is not *enough*. Or, rather, life-enhancement sits too easily with consumer culture, as if living a life of faith is simply a matter of working on one's own individual well-being.

In accepting the challenge that Dedji offers, though, we could look at things the other way round. Our lives *will* be enhanced if we become disciples of Christ. We open ourselves up to life-changing experiences and a changed future if we wholeheartedly inhabit the story that God is telling in Christ. We do not inhabit the story as a self-improvement exercise. We do so because it is right and just and true. Any enhancement or enrichment we may enjoy are but by-products. There are, almost certainly, also going to be struggles, pain, hassle, opposition. No one ever said the way of Christ was easy.

Inter-generational wisdom

One further, vital observation about faith communities as carriers of God's story is necessary: they are inter-generational. Wisdom does not inevitably come with age, but communal wisdom will not come without some of the wisdom of years. Wisdom is likely to reside in the views and insights of people of a wide range of ages, and in the midst of their conversations. Elihu is one of the conversation-partners of Job. He accepts that he is not very old, but nevertheless believes he has things to say, and challenges the notion that it is only the old that are wise. Rather, 'it is the spirit in a mortal, the breath of the Almighty, that makes for understanding' (Job 32:8). A crucial conclusion to be drawn from this exchange is that it is from the interaction of generational insights that wisdom emerges. Churches (and other communities of faith) are not the only examples in Western culture of inter-generational communities outside of families, but they are key, and quite unusual, contexts in which different generations meet and interact constructively and creatively.

There are important lessons to be learned by churches

from the way in which the use of stories, and the process of reflecting on life stories turns experiences into testimony. A recent exercise in the British Methodist Church invited older members of the church to write a letter to a younger member. They would not know who received the letter, yet all letter-writers knew that their letters could be read out in public, as well as being received by someone between the age of 8 and 23 somewhere in Britain. The full contents of all those letters have still to be studied, yet they were full of hope, if wistful at times. Often nostalgic and reflective, the writers frequently recalled what had helped them in their youth to discover God/Jesus/Christ experientially, or to be inspired to see the Gospel's full richness with respect to the whole of life.

Words from the old to the young need to be cautiously framed lest the implication is that there is a set way of doing things, a particular style which has to be followed, or specific words which should always be used. Starting the other way round means encouraging children and young people, and those (of any age) who are new to faith to use the words which come naturally as they encounter and explore the things of faith (and the Christian story) for the first time. Yet again we are to remind each other to 'tell it like it is', not as we think it has to be told.

The reservoir is there to be drawn from by seekers and believers of any age and background. The challenge is to ensure that access to the reservoir is enabled for all, including those of different social and ethnic backgrounds and different educational abilities. Lillian Daniel tells a powerful story of a children's worker who did not want to tell her own testimony to the children she taught in the church. Her testimony was best offered to the adults. In that way the younger people saw that testimony-giving was something to aspire to. Children and young people can (must!) be supported in their growth, including in faith, in the church. Too often those who have grown to adulthood within church have not been enabled to see how faith continues to develop beyond childhood and youth. Parents are guilty of implying this whenever they suggest that you 'learn good morals' through Religious Education in schools, or in church, as if spirituality comprises only ethics. Whilst recognizing that faith is something for every life stage, it has to keep on developing in adult life. Its expression and exploration lie at the heart of the wisdom held, supported and drawn from within the church as a living, story-carrying, inter-generational community.

POINT OF REFLECTION

Have a think about the life stage you are at. In what ways do you link up with those of other generations – older or younger? With whom do you talk about your faith? From whom do you most expect to learn? From whom *have* you learned?

PRAYER
Creative God,
you have given us a melody to work with.
Gather round us, we pray, all the
musicians we need to make great music.
Let others shine.
Let us have our moment, too.
For you.

Chapter 12

LIVING THE STORY: ON BEING COMMITTED

In the second of our two 'rounding off' chapters, Barbara writes about vocation: 'I am a Methodist Minister. This is not my job but my vocation; it is who I am. In this final section I not only want to reflect on the story so far but also to remember and give thanks for the people and communities that have consistently and sacrificially "watched over me with love".'

If I think of the stories that called me into ministry then I would begin with Sally Trench's, *Bury Me in My Boots*.[1] The book tells the story of a woman who left behind a privileged upbringing to work alongside the street homeless of London and with children excluded from school. It was probably the first radical story that I heard and, whilst it is now very dated, at the time it was an important stepping stone on my path towards ministry. The Biblical story that went alongside it was the story of the Father who waits, then known as 'the Prodigal Son' but later understood differently. The overarching text, learned for a Bible Exam, was that 'Nothing can separate us from the love of God in Christ Jesus' and embracing this was a sense of being loved by my family, my church and, by deduction, ultimately by the one who had created me in the first place.

But maybe more influential were the stories told in the everyday actions of people around me, not least Jill Bowden, a lively, moped riding, left-wing Deaconess, sent to wake up a complacent South of England congregation and work with 'the youth'. She embodied for me, something intriguing enough to change the direction of my life. When I think about 'Living the Christian story', Jill, Sally, the Lost Son are all characters in the script, talking to and with each other in the layers of story that unfolded. Of course, there are many other characters too including some villains. Layer upon layer of encounter, learning and Bible text, forming and reforming experience and ministry. If I were to try to think of a gastronomic analogy to this process I would say that it's more like noodles than mille-feuille (for the gastronomically illiterate – more of a tangle of threads than a sweet, neatly layered pastry!)

What this dish of life's noodles has taught me is that being human is complicated, and, to continue with the analogy, it's better to savour the dish than to try to disentangle it. Stories move around each other, inform each other, contradict each other and yet somehow ultimately form something that is richer and more satisfying. We need to be fearful neither of complexity nor contradiction in our endeavours to hold fast to that which is good. To see that something is complicated, is not to admit defeat, but rather to recognise the nuance and unfinished nature of human narrative. Acknowledging complexity enables us to resist stereo-typing, to honour the contradictory nature of human experience, to see each other as unfinished manifestations of God's continuing, creative interaction with the World.

Incarnation

To be a Christian minister, is to say 'yes' to a covenant relationship with the Church. This covenant gives both security and responsibility. At the Reception into Full Connexion, a Methodist Presbyter makes promises to abide within the discipline of the Church and in turn the Church promises to take care of the Presbyter, it is about relationship or as Methodists rather quaintly put it, 'watching over one another in love'. Like all relationships this can have pros and cons. Ordained ministry is a public role, and as such has particular responsibilities that might not be personal preferences. On the other hand, it is a hugely privileged position, opening doors to many people especially at times of personal crisis or bereavement. Ministry is never 'just a job' but always a way of being, something that affects every level of our lives, something through which we are formed. For all ministry (lay and ordained) the call to discipleship is about putting our bodies where our beliefs are, standing alongside, or in solidarity with, those who need us most.

As I have grown into ministry, I have seen the intimate link between Christmas and Easter. These two major festivals are no longer 'stand-alone' events, one where we remember Jesus as a baby and the other his death and resurrection. On the contrary, I see that death and resurrection are also about incarnation – that life and death are part of the same package. And I have realised that God's incarnate presence is inherent in all that life brings to us. God is not flown in for special occasions, but is part of the warp and weft of all life, God is with us always. This sense of having God immanently among us, has sustained my ministry and I have come to interpret God's apparent silences as times of profound listening to the birth pangs of the World.

POINT OF CONNECTION

Is there an individual or book that was a turning point in your journey of faith? Have you ever told them? In turn, I wonder whose memory holds your testimony?

POINT OF REFLECTION

The story of Pentecost at the beginning of Acts is often hailed as the birthday of the Church but maybe we should also hail it as the beginning of understanding? It was not so much that people spoke in different tongues, but that they were understood by those around them. This story, above all others is about listening differently and understanding what is being said in an atmosphere of complexity. Is it possible that reading this story with new eyes might give the Church another birthday?

Transformation

This ministerial formation, has often been a transformation. That is, the gospel has jolted me into fresh understanding of both life and in turn life has shaken me to revisit the gospel. That is, the pattern of reflection between experience, Scripture, reason and tradition encouraged by the Methodist quadrilateral has sometimes spiralled in unexpected directions. In particular I have been deeply challenged in relation to the stories of LGBTQI Christians who I have encountered along the way. I recognise in the accounts of their 'coming out' a description of a transformative process that both challenges and potentially transforms the Church.

This transformative process is something like this. 'I am not who others think that I am', 'I have no idea who I am', 'I wonder if I could be this?', 'I am this', 'This is who I am!'. This process of coming out can take a lifetime and can often involve a complete breakdown of self-identity. Coming out stories are invariably painful and involve a coming out to self, 'I am this', as well as a coming out to others 'This is who I am!' And for many in the gay community it is an on-going process of testing whether or not it is safe to make disclosures of sexuality or gender. Sadly, too often it is not safe.

Stories of transformation run through New Testament text at every turn. From people who thought they were fishermen, turning on their heels to follow a Messiah, to diffident disciples making declarations about the Kingdom and zealous Pharisees setting sail as missionaries. Jesus himself asks the disciples, 'Who do others say that I am?' and rips the curtain between earth and heaven as his true self is revealed, the beloved Son, incarnate and transcendent, human and divine.

I see this story threading through history as we have lived our story, and then re-visited the stories we tell of it. In particular in the Methodist Church of today, we find ourselves in transformation, asking 'Who do people say that we are?' and trying to articulate again what our unique message is for the current World. As we have lost confidence in the old ways and see the need to change, we are also in the uncomfortable place of losing our identity and searching for who we are meant to become. We are not what we thought we were and as we seek to become something different we must live through the chaos and loss of identity which requires both faith and courage. By its very nature, transformation is not something we can control and if the church is to 'come out' then we will need to live through an uncomfortable process that will challenge us to the core. As we live through this process and wonder whether in fact the church is able to survive and become something new, I see some glimpses of hope.

Prophetic action

Prophets read the signs of the times to call God's people back to ways of justice and righteousness. They are often speaking against prevalent narratives and as such can bring an unpopular message. They speak out of love for their people, even though they are often exasperated, they are not mavericks but steeped in a tradition, knowing and understanding yet also looking beyond the present. They are a troubling presence.

Whilst individual prophets may be few and far between, prophetic communities are more common and we see them emerging both within and outside faith communities. Some such have been Outcome and Dignity and Worth within the Methodist Church's struggle with understanding sexuality, gender and relationships. One glimpse of great hope has been the call to live as 'a fellowship of controversy'. This phrase has been a reminder to the church that, whilst we will probably never reach consensus on same-sex marriage, we need to let our love for each other make a climate of listening and learning. As we begin to understand what it will mean for us to live with contradictory convictions, these prophetic groups have spearheaded an approach that can move us away from confrontational binary argument and to a sense of Christian maturity that allows for human story to be nuanced and contradictory without losing sight of the gospel.

Similarly, the work of the Joint Public Issues Team has enabled informed conversations around food poverty and Universal Credit and many other social issues, which has moved us to challenge political assumptions as well as providing 'first aid' through food banks and provision for the homeless.

The Survivor Reference group has challenged the church to wake up to the effects of abuse following the Past Cases Review and is active in advocating worship and safe space within the church to the benefit of all.

The Activist network connects those involved with lobbying and demonstrating to challenge inequalities and visibly to stand beside marginalised groups. It was good to see the London District coming out with their banner 'We are Methodist' at a recent demonstration.

These are but a few of a bubbling up of prophetic voices, calling the church to declare, 'This is who we are!'

Connexional communities

Potentially one of the great strengths of the Methodist Church is our Connexionalism, that is we are all connected to each other in a network, Ministers are itinerant, properties are held in common and every Church member should belong to a small group or class. Of course, at our worst, we are inclined to squander this by being parochial, fighting for 'our' resources and being territorial.

Across all denominations there has been a re-visiting of new monasticism. Historically we have lost our sense of monastic community and moved towards a more established model of Church. In doing so we have often lost a sense of being bound by a way of life, common values and responsibilities. New monasticism calls us back to patterns of accountability within which we can be recalled to 'watch over one another with love'.

At the Methodist Conference of 2018 there was discussion about a Methodist Way of Life, and whilst this would not preclude other Rules of Life of a more ecumenical nature, it was a sign of hope that we could revisit the heart of what it means to be Methodist.

Some churches and house groups are adopting this way of life, others are seeking to live in gathered or dispersed communities. This groundswell of interest seems to be at the heart of who we are becoming and it will be good to hear the stories of these communities as they grow and learn together.

POINT OF CONNECTION
This section has been unapologetically 'Methodist', I wonder what points your particular tradition echoes these reflections and what we might share ecumenically that would enrich all our traditions?

POINT OF REFLECTION
If you were to write a 'Way of Life' to reflect your priorities as an individual or within a community, what would be essential and how could you 'watch over each other with love'?

So what's the story?
The question has a hint of accusation about it. How are we to give account of being people of faith 'for just such a time as this'? We are surrounded by information, through many different types of media. We are recipients of 'fake news' and 'spin'. We live in a bewildering morass of political unrest both at home and internationally. We have to face our colonial past and acknowledge our new place in history. We live amongst people of many different faiths, and people

who despise or are indifferent to religion. We are called to be Christians in a strange landscape, in fragile communities and aging congregations. Yet we are still called to 'hold fast to that which is good.'

We also know, that as Christians we are accountable to God. Not that we should bear unnecessary guilt for all the world's troubles, rather that we should be seeking always to love our neighbours and our enemies, to speak ill of no one, to protect creation and to strive for justice and peace for all humanity. It is of course an impossible task for us on our own, but it is nevertheless an imperative for all who seek to follow Jesus. Unlike most projects that require us to quantify our outcomes, we are never sure how we are getting along. What we think might be pleasing and righteousness might, with hindsight appear to have been misguided or shallow. What we think might have been a waste of time, might in fact have been transformative or life-saving in ways we could never have anticipated. We can only strive towards these ends and start over when we mess up, assured that we are not only accountable to but also held in loving attention by a God of grace.

We are called into this great love story with God, a story that spans not just our lives but the whole of eternity. We are both the main character and a walk on part. Our narrative intertwines and connects with the great Biblical themes of creation, redemption, death, resurrection, judgement and salvation. It calls us into life in all its fullness, its despair and elation, its chaos and delight. It is a story about what happens ultimately, one in which we are all caught up until God the Author writes the final chapters and calls all creation home.

This is a book, that having written, we need to write again and again because there is so much more to be said and learned, so much more to understand and re-visit. For now, this is the story.

POINT OF CONNECTION

If you were asked to lead your church for one year only, what would be the one thing you would want to say?

POINT OF REFLECTION

One of the great treasures of the Methodist tradition is the Covenant Service. Every year members of the Methodist Church will renew our promise to live our lives remembering, not only our commitments but also the faithfulness of God's love for us. At the heart of this service is the Covenant Prayer (taken from the Methodist Worship Book):

I am no longer my own but yours.
Put me to what you will, rank me with whom you will;
put me to doing, put me to suffering;
let me be employed for you, or laid aside for you,
exalted for you, or brought low for you;
let me be full, let me be empty,
let me have all things, let me have nothing:
I freely and wholeheartedly yield all things
to your pleasure and disposal.
And now, glorious and blessèd God, Father, Son and Holy Spirit,
you are mine and I am yours.
And the covenant now made on earth, let it be ratified in heaven. Amen.

How can we take the next step in our covenant relationship with God?

PRAYER

I pray,
That should I ever be accused of being a
Christian
By those who wish to harm me
That if my words or courage fail me
My face, my heart, my actions
Would betray me
And that I would have the faith
To live my life, every day
Knowing that God is my only judge
Constantly watching over me with love.

P.S. I am happy to be buried in my boots. Barbara

FOR FOLLOWING UP

This is a list of suggestions of things you might follow up if you were especially interested in the themes of particular chapters. We haven't tried to 'grade' them in terms of levels of difficulty, and some of the books listed are big, others small. We merely want you to take your enthusiasms further, bearing in mind one basic rule: there is absolutely *nothing* that you *have* to read to follow up this book. Only follow through what you are likely to enjoy, and be inspired by.

1. Aesop, *Fables* (many editions).
    Christopher Booker, *The Seven Basic Plots: Why We Tell Stories* (Bloomsbury 2005).
    J. M. Coetzee and Arabella Kurtz, *The Good Story: Exchanges on Truth, Fiction and Psychotherapy* (Vintage 2016).
    Richard Kearney, *On Stories* (Routledge 2002).
    Yann Martel, *Life of Pi* (Knopf 2001) [Film version, dir. Ang Lee, 2012.]

2. Barbara Glasson, *I am Somewhere Else* (Darton, Longman and Todd 2006).
    Clive Marsh, *Christianity in a Post-Atheist Age* (London: SCM Press 2002), Ch.1.

3. Tim Dowley ed., *A Short Introduction to the History of Christianity* (Fortress Press 2018).

Luke Timothy Johnson, *The New Testament: A Very Short Introduction* (Oxford University Press 2010).

Alister E. McGrath, *Christian Theology: An Introduction 6th edition* (Wiley-Blackwell 2016).

Tony Lane, *A Concise History of Christian Thought Revised edn.* (Baker Academic 2006)

Robert Bruce Mullin, *A Short World History of Christianity* (Westminster John Knox Press 2014).

Frederick W. Norris, *Christianity: A Short Global History* (Oneworld 2002).

John Riches, *The Bible: A Very Short Introduction* (Oxford University Press 2000).

Linda Woodhead, *Christianity: A Very Short Introduction 2nd edition* (Oxford University Press 2014).

4.   Lillian Daniel, *Tell it Like it is: Reclaiming the Practice of Testimony* (Rowman & Littlefield/Alban Books 2005), Thomas G. Long, *Testimony: Talking Ourselves into being Christian* (Jossey Bass 2004).

5.   Barbara Glasson, *A Spirituality of Survival: Enabling a response to trauma and abuse* (London: Mowbray 2009).

TV Mini-series, *Patrick Melrose* (Sky Atlantic 2018).

PODS Web-site (Positive Outcomes for Dissociative Survivors), https://www.pods-online.org.uk/

6.   Richard Burridge, *Four Gospels, One Jesus?: A Symbolic Reading 2nd edition* (SPCK 2005).

Dorothee Soelle and Luise Schottroff, *Jesus of Nazareth* (SPCK 2002).

Marcus J. Borg and N.T. Wright, *The Meaning of Jesus: Two Visions Revised edition* (HarperOne 2007).

Symon Hill, *The Upside-Down Bible: What Jesus*

Really Said about Money, Sex and Violence (Darton, Longman and Todd 2015).

Clive Marsh and Steve Moyise, *Jesus and the Gospels* 3rd*edition*. Bloomsbury 2015).

J. L. Houlden, *Jesus: A Question of Identity* (Continuum 2005).

The New Testament Gateway, http://www.ntgateway. com/

7. Kenneth E. Bailey, *Jesus through Middle Eastern Eyes* (Inter-Varsity Press 2008).
    The Eagle Huntress (dir. Otto Bell, 2016; DVD: Altitude Film Distribution 2017).
    Barbara Glasson, *Eating Curry for Heaven's Sake* (Kevin Mayhew 2015).
    Howard A. Snyder and Joel Scandrett, *Salvation Means Creation Healed: The Ecology of Sin and Grace* (Cascade Books 2011).

8. Frank Barron, Alfonso Montuori and Anthea Barron eds., *Creators on Creating: Awakening and Cultivating the Imaginative Mind* (Jeremy P. Tarcher/Penguin 1997).
    Gordon D. Kaufman, *In the beginning... Creativity* (Augsburg Fortress Press 2000).
    Doris Salcedo *Shibboleth* (Tate Shots), available at: https://www.youtube.com/watch?v=NlJDn2MAn9I
    The Year of Anish Kapoor (BBC TV, *Imagine* series; Series 9, Episode 1; 2011).
    Jeanette Winterson, *Art Objects: Essays on Ecstasy and Effrontery* (Vintage 1996).

9. Dwight N. Hopkins and George C. L. Cummings eds., *Cut Loose Your Stammering Tongue: Black Theology in the Slave Narrative 2nd edn.* (Westminster John Knox Press 2003).

Michael Jagessar and Anthony Reddie, *Postcolonial Black British Theology: New Textures and Themes* (Peterborough: Epworth Press 2007).

Barbara Kingsolver, *The Poisonwood Bible* (Harper 1998, and later edns.).

Andrea Levy, *Small Island* (Headline Publishing Group 2004).

10. Andrew Porter, *Religion Versus Empire?: British Protestant Missionaries and Overseas Expansion, 1700-1914* (Manchester University Press 2004).

Brian Stanley, *The Bible and the Flag: Protestant missions and British imperialism in the nineteenth and twentieth centuries* (Apollos 1990).

Phyllis Trible, *Texts of Terror: Literary-Feminist Readings of Biblical Narrative* (SCM Press 2011; original 1984); Preface by Revd Dr Jane Craske.

11. Clive Marsh, *Christ in Practice: A Christology of Everyday Life* (Darton, Longman and Todd 2006).

Paul and Sally Nash, *Tools for Reflective Ministry* (SPCK 2012).

Vaughan S. Roberts and David Sims, *Leading by Story: Rethinking Church Leadership* (SCM Press 2017).

Roger Walton, *The Reflective Disciple* (SCM Press 2012).

12. Barbara Glasson, *The Exuberant Church: Listening to the Prophetic People of God* (Darton, Longman and Todd 2011).

Mary Grey, *Prophecy and Mysticism: Prophetic Heart of the Postmodern Church* (T&T Clark 1997).

Jane Leach and Michael Paterson, *Pastoral Supervision: A Handbook* 2nd edn. (SCM Press 2015).

NOTES

CHAPTER 4
1. Lillian Daniel, *Tell it Like it is: Reclaiming the Practice of Testimony* (Rowman & Littlefield/Alban Books 2005), p.12.
2. Daniel, *Tell it Like it is*, p.160.
3. Daniel, *Tell it Like it is*, p.13.
4. Daniel, *Tell it Like it is*, p.21.

CHAPTER 5
1. Riet Bons-Storm, *The Incredible Woman: Listening to Women's Silences in Pastoral Care and Counselling* (Abingdon Press 1996), p.122.
2. Joan Laird, 'Women and Stories: Restorying Women's Self Constructions', in Monica McGoldrick, Carol M. Anderson and Froma Walsh, eds., *Women in Families: A Framework of Family Therapy* (Norton 1991), p.430.
3. Bons-Storm, *The Incredible Woman*, p.58.
4. *Time for Action: Sexual abuse, the Churches and a new dawn for survivors* (CTBI 2002).

CHAPTER 6
1. Adapted from the prayer 'Images', inspired by the work of John A.T. Robinson, in George Appleton, *One Man's Prayers* (2nd edn.) (SPCK 1977).

CHAPTER 7
1. *Dialogue and Proclamation: Reflections and Orientations on Interreligious Dialogue and the Proclamation of the Gospel of Jesus Christ*. Pontifical Council for Interreligious Dialogue and Congregation for the Evangelization of the Peoples 1991; available at: http://www.vatican.va/roman_curia/pontifical_

councils/interelg/documents/rc_pc_interelg_doc_19051991_
dialogue-and-proclamatio_en.html

2. *Acting in God's Love: Christian Witness in a Multi-Religious World*, collated by Bonnie Evans Hill and Barbara Glasson (CTBI Interfaith Theological Advisory Group 2018), available at: http://www.presenceandengagement.org.uk/sites/default/files/Acting-in-Gods-Love-Christian-Witness-in-a-Multi-Religious-World.pdf

3. Howard A. Snyder and Joel Scandrett, *Salvation Means Creation Healed: The Ecology of Sin and Grace* (Cascade Books 2011).

CHAPTER 8

1. Jeanette Winterson, *Art Objects: Essays on Ecstasy and Effrontery* (Vintage 1996) p.142.

2. Annie Dillard, 'Heaven and Earth in Jest' in Frank Barron, Alfonso Montuori and Anthea Barron eds., *Creators on Creating: Awakening and Cultivating the Imaginative Mind* (Jeremy P. Tarcher/Penguin 1997), p.85.

CHAPTER 9

1. *The Guardian* newspaper (22 November 2018).

CHAPTER 10

1. *A Report on Church, State and Establishment*, Received by the Methodist Conference of 2004, https://www.methodist.org.uk/downloads/pi_churchstateestablishment_04.pdf (accessed 27th January 2019).

CHAPTER 11

1. Valentin Dedji, 'Holiness, grace and mission: revisiting John Wesley's missiological mandate' (*Holiness* 1.2 (2015), available at: https://www.wesley.cam.ac.uk/holiness/archive-issues/holiness-mission/ (accessed 16th January 2019).

CHAPTER 12

1. Sally Trench, *Bury Me in My Boots* (Hodder and Stoughton 1968).